KARMA
CAPITALISM

KARMA CAPITALISM

WHY BEING A GOOD BUSINESS *IS* GOOD BUSINESS

JAMES REED

EBURY EDGE

UK | USA | Canada | Ireland | Australia
India | New Zealand | South Africa

Ebury Edge is part of the Penguin Random House group of companies
whose addresses can be found at global.penguinrandomhouse.com

Penguin Random House UK
One Embassy Gardens, 8 Viaduct Gardens, London SW11 7BW

penguin.co.uk
global.penguinrandomhouse.com

First published by Ebury Edge in 2025

I

Photography by Harry Reed, Stefan Gatt and Michael Woods

Typeset in 11.75/14.2 pt Dante MT Pro by Six Red Marbles UK, Thetford, Norfolk

Printed and bound in Great Britain by Clays Ltd, Elcograf S.p.A.

The authorised representative in the EEA is Penguin Random House Ireland,
Morrison Chambers, 32 Nassau Street, Dublin D02 YH68

A CIP catalogue record for this book is available from the British Library

ISBN 9781529147223

Penguin Random House is committed to a sustainable future
for our business, our readers and our planet. This book is made
from Forest Stewardship Council® certified paper.

For my father and all the other Karma Capitalists
who decide to share this journey

CONTENTS

Introduction
My defining moment: A wake-up fall 1

PART ONE A happy accident 15
1. What is a PhilCo? 17

PART TWO The burning platform:
Capitalism in crisis 31
2. What's the point of business? 33
3. The time for action is now 51
4. The ESG delusion 65

PART THREE The case for real change 87
5. In search of . . . longevity 89
6. Strengthening the brand 109

PART FOUR How to create a PhilCo 133
7. Choosing the right model 135
8. Establishing a charitable foundation 157
9. How to spend it 171

PART FIVE Let's do it 191
10. Become a PhilCo 193
11. Frequently asked questions (FAQs) 203

Afterword 211
Glossary 213
Appendix 217
References 219
Acknowledgements 231
Index 233

INTRODUCTION
MY DEFINING MOMENT: A WAKE-UP FALL

One day, not so long ago, I had a visitor from the Harvard Business School. Professor Lauren Cohen is an expert in entrepreneurial finance and family businesses. Just before he left, he asked a great question.

'What is the defining moment of your career so far?'

It is not often that I am stumped. I've been the CEO of Reed since 1997, a role that involves doing countless interviews with newspapers, TV and radio. And then there are the thousands of questions I am asked every year by the team, who need me to respond with a firm decision. *This is what we'll do. This will be our direction of travel.*

The defining moment in my career so far? Could there be such a thing? Just one moment? Dozens of scenarios flooded into my mind. Was it the time we received a tax bill out of the blue that ran to nine figures? Or the time, in 1995, when we took a leap of faith and started Britain's first employment website? Or the time I caught one of the finance team with their hand in the till? There were lots of contenders, but none quite fitted the bill as *the* defining moment so far.

Then, quite unexpectedly, the answer came to me and suddenly there were no other possibilities at all. Funnily enough, this moment did not take place in the office, or anywhere to do with work. It was about as far away from a corporate setting as you can be.

The moment came in the Alps in 2013, on a climbing trip to the Matterhorn, which straddles the border between Switzerland and Italy. It's probably the most photographed mountain in the world, immortalised by Toblerone. I had just turned 50 and I was with my son Harry, who had just turned 18. As well as celebrating these landmark birthdays, the trip was going to be a father-and-son bonding exercise.

We travelled in September, for one reason: to avoid thunderstorms. Fierce thunderstorms can be a hazard in the Alps in the summer. I had developed an acute fear of them after coming rather too close to being struck by lightning on two alpine expeditions, to the Dent du Géant and Piz Badile mountains. Both those trips had been in July, unlike this one, but there was one constant. My mountain guide every time was Stefan Gatt, a famous alpinist who was also the first person to snowboard down Everest. (He climbed it without oxygen and took his father with him.) For the trip with Harry and me, he was accompanied by his expert colleague and friend Markus Stockert.

On the Matterhorn, things did not bode well from the beginning. There had been a fresh snowfall and it all looked very lovely, like a fluffy white blanket. But beneath the snow were patches of hardened ice that had survived the heatwave earlier that summer. They made the mountain hazardous and slippery. Effectively, even though it was only September, we were climbing the Matterhorn from the less frequented and more technical Italian side in winter conditions. We had elected to climb the Lion Ridge with its beautiful rock formations and in theory shorter distance to the summit. The downside is that this route can be more exposed to harsh weather conditions. Just to add to our discomfort, the wind had come up, making one side of the ridge we were climbing bitterly cold. The higher we climbed, the colder it got.

The day before, we had passed the cemetery in Zermatt and stopped to pay our respects to the climbers who are buried there. Almost 600 alpinists have lost their lives climbing the Matterhorn, making it one of the deadliest peaks in the world. There are fatalities every season, most of which are caused by sudden changes in the weather and climbing errors. The first ascent of the Matterhorn, led by Edward Whymper

in 1865, ended in tragedy when four climbers who were roped
together fell to their death on the way down.

The first time I fell, it was like a scene from a thriller
except, believe me, it's no fun when you're the star of the
movie. I was edging myself cautiously across a snow slope
when I lost my footing, slipped and started to slide towards a
sheer drop, dragging Stefan, whom I was roped to, down with
me. For a few moments, the suddenness of the fall and speed
of the slide disorientated me. The crampons on my boots,
spiked attachments that were meant to act as brakes, didn't
bite. Then somehow, I remembered the ice axe that had been
secured across my chest. I turned the sharp end into the ice
and as I slid pressed all my weight down upon it. The axe did
its job and I managed to stop the fall, about a metre from the
edge and the long drop below. Stefan was able to stop too,

5

thankfully. Time stood still as, side by side, we just looked at each other. Then, very carefully, we climbed back up to safety.

Even now, I vividly remember the feeling of being totally focused in that moment. It was as if my whole being knew that I had one job – to stop the fall. I now understand what people mean when they talk about a state of flow, or a state of absolute focus.

I know it's a bit of a cliché but, in life-or-death moments like this, everything really did seem to happen in slow motion. I was fully aware of each agonising second. I also felt another presence that I can't explain, as if a gentle hand stopped me sliding over the edge. Harry told me later that a hand had played a part for him too – a real one. As I fell, Markus, his climbing companion, reached over and turned Harry's head, so that he was facing away from the scene and wouldn't see what happened next.

I have often been asked why, after the first near-fatal fall, we decided to continue climbing at all. It's hard to explain beyond a certain bull-headed determination to do what we had set out to do. A decade earlier I had successfully climbed Mont Blanc; to my mind, the Matterhorn, which is a beautiful and iconic peak, was the perfect bookend to a decade of alpinism. It did not occur to me that the time might not be right, that this expedition might be ill-starred, that the mountain had not given us permission on this occasion to climb it.

We didn't succeed in reaching the top. After more than eight hours climbing and within sight of the summit, we took the decision to turn back to spend the night in a high-altitude hut we had passed earlier that afternoon. The weather was worsening. The biting wind, which had already turned my fingers into blocks of ice, was reaching dangerous speeds and the temperature was falling fast. It seemed sensible to hunker down in the safety of the hut. Climbing into my sleeping bag,

I took a crumb of comfort from the news that we were too high for rats and mice because this looked like just the kind of place where they would have felt at home. The next day, after we had finally decided to turn our back on the Matterhorn, to descend and go home, I fell again. This time I was abseiling. I found myself at the end of a long rope, having descended one cliff edge and then crossed a shallower slope to join Stefan. Unfortunately, the length of the rope and my unsteady weight at the end of it precipitated what is known as a pendulum fall. The person at the end of the rope is not suspended in a straight line from the anchor point. So the climber does not fall downwards, but instead swings uncontrollably. On a mountainside this can have disastrous consequences. Swept from one side to the other, the climber is at risk of colliding with every sharp piece of rock.

I tried to use my feet as brakes as I felt myself being dragged to the right but could not stop myself. After swinging for what felt like an eternity, I ended up dangling over a sheer drop. I could see that my right leg was broken. I knew this because my foot was pointing in the wrong direction.

Stefan managed to pull me back to a ledge before calling the air ambulance. Luckily the wind had abated by now and I was saved by an Italian mountain rescue crew. One of them was winched down from the helicopter to assist me. 'My name is Roberta,' she said. 'Would you like to speak Italian, French, German or English?' I thought she was an angel, and I still do.

During my recovery, there was plenty of time to reflect on this experience – in hospital, in bed at home, then in a wheelchair pushed by my wife Nicola (who may have been rolling her eyes). My instinct had been to call the expedition my double fail. Not only did we fail to get to the top of the mountain, we then failed to get to the bottom. When I thought harder, though, I realised that I had been given a

second chance, or even, as I'd fallen twice, a third one. I had survived two near-death experiences in the space of 24 hours. This was not something that could be ignored.

Thinking about that first fall, even now, more than a decade later, still makes me feel nauseous. I came inches away from killing myself and my friend. The image is seared in my mind. The whole experience is like a film I mentally revisit again and again. I have no doubt that my time on the Matterhorn profoundly changed me. Life, its value and its fragility became so much more vivid. I had a sense that I should now live differently.

It wasn't just that I promised Nicola that I would give up climbing. I wanted to make sure that I made the most of the time I had left, however little that might be. I became much more focused on my purpose as a person and, equally, on the purpose of Reed, the company I run. I felt a surge of new life and new energy, but where should I direct it? What was the problem or problems that most needed solving?

I became more acutely aware of how we, as humans, are so dependent on one another and started to think more intensely about what we might do for other people. I resolved to become much more involved in the activities of our charity, Big Give. And, after a while, after engaging with input from across our group, we settled on Reed's company purpose of 'improving lives through work'. This has been our guiding principle ever since. My work today is defined by my desire to deliver it, to be a purpose-driven business leader and to maximise our philanthropic impact through Big Give. I doubt I would have become so focused on how I might be able to help others if it hadn't been for that ill-fated trip.

There is some grim irony in the fact that my father, Alec Reed, also had his own brush with death, his own defining moment in his early fifties, that set Reed on the path to becoming a PhilCo, or Philanthropy Company. I remember it clearly. One Saturday, not long after the New Year in 1986, he asked me to sit down with him in the family kitchen because he had something important to tell me. I knew immediately from his expression that it was serious.

My father told me that he had been diagnosed with colon cancer and that he would be going into hospital the following week for an operation to remove the tumour. He said he had been feeling unwell for some time, but his symptoms had been previously dismissed by several doctors who felt his sickness was largely 'in the mind'. But his problem, he said, was not in the mind. It was in the gut. It was not until he saw Dr Ken Kwok that he received his diagnosis. He was 51 at the time. Hearing all this, I remember experiencing a rising sense of panic. Unsure what to do, I went straight to the village church to pray for his recovery.

What my father didn't tell me on that Saturday in January was that his cancer was stage 4 and he had been given a 40 per cent chance of survival. However, his doctor had also told him that if he lived for five years, he would most likely be clear of the cancer. So Alec Reed the accountant went to work. There are 60 months in 5 years and there was a 60 per cent chance he would not make it. He then divided one number into the other and concluded he had a 1 per cent chance of dying each month. This was a manageable risk, he thought, and one he would do all that he could to avoid. His coping mechanism wouldn't have won him a maths prize but psychologically it was genius.

The operation the following week appeared to go well. A large section of my father's colon was successfully removed but the procedure left a deep scar on his stomach. After surgery, he began a long period of convalescence and was nursed tirelessly by my mother Adrianne. It was her belief that my father's cancer had been caused by stress and she was determined to remedy the situation. At the time Reed, his principal company, had been through a turbulent time, narrowly avoiding disaster in a recent recession. His subsidiary company, the drugstore chain Medicare, was still struggling to make a profit. He had been working all hours and at weekends. He had not been sleeping. He was exhausted.

My mother decided that my father must reduce his workload and told him to sell Medicare to make his life more manageable. My father was in no state to disagree and the board supported my mother's decision. The investment bank Hill Samuel was appointed to run the process and to elicit interest from potential trade buyers. They did a good job and by early summer there were three interested parties. It was agreed that the company would be sold by a sealed bid auction, whereby each prospective buyer submits their best bid in a sealed envelope and the highest bid wins. Two of the bids were quite close together, offering in the region of £12 million, but the third bidder, the Dee Group, came in considerably higher at £20 million. My mother was vindicated, and Hill Samuel had earned their fee. My father, who owned a quarter of the business, received £5 million in cash.

With the shadow of his cancer still looming, my father wondered what he should do with such a sizeable sum. Much of it, he feared, would disappear in taxes, especially as he had been told it was more likely than not that he would die, at which point death duty and capital gains tax would apply. After much consideration, he decided to give the money to charity.

The charity he decided to give the money to was one he had created when he had first floated Reed. Reed Charity had since supported several initiatives, especially around the rehabilitation of drug addicts, but this latest substantial donation gave it a whole new range of possibilities. Not long after, the opportunity arose to buy a 10 per cent stake in Reed Executive, the company he had founded. So, in 1986, Reed Charity became a significant shareholder in Reed Executive.

At the time no one, including my father, realised the significance of this. However, it is fundamentally true to say that this was the moment when our company's DNA changed. The charity was now embedded in the company. It was years later before we realised this change had given our company a new strength, a new superpower that better equipped it to go out and meet the challenges and opportunities of the future.

Now, almost 40 years later, my mission is to build on my father's legacy, to share how the PhilCo experience has worked so well for us and for others and to encourage you to find renewed purpose in your own work through the PhilCo movement. Together we can change the DNA of business. We will do so one company at a time and, by doing so, we can ultimately change the DNA of capitalism itself.

This is my ambition. This is my objective. This is my reason for writing this book. And yes, I do plan to send a copy to Roberta. But first, what exactly is a PhilCo? Why are they such a good thing? And why is it that we need to change the DNA of capitalism?

PART ONE
A HAPPY ACCIDENT

1
WHAT IS A PHILCO?

PHILCOS DELIVER BETTER RESULTS, LAST LONGER AND ARE TYPICALLY GREAT PLACES TO WORK

Purpose has been at the heart of my family since my father, Alec, opened the first office of Reed Employment back in 1960, later establishing the Reed Foundation in 1986. Today that foundation owns 18 per cent of the Reed Group and has financed thousands of charitable initiatives. We are best known for Big Give, which by the spring of 2025 has used match-funding campaigns to raise more than £350 million for thousands of different charities. By 2030, the aim is to have raised £1 billion.

At Reed we did not arrive where we are today by design; it was more of a happy accident. We survived, we adapted and we experimented with new models. Our current model and PhilCo status arose from a family crisis, a sequence of unforeseen events that led to my father donating £5 million to charity, which enabled that charity to buy shares in the business he founded. It has been proven again and again that the PhilCo business model is robust. PhilCos deliver better results, last longer and are typically great places to work. They also have a reach that goes way beyond the immediate business as they contribute to society more widely.

But what exactly is a PhilCo? Let me give you my best shot at a definition. In short, a PhilCo is a Philanthropy Company, or a business that is partially owned by a charitable foundation. After consulting with owners and leaders of similar businesses, I have settled on a simple definition that has wide support and approval:

A PhilCo is a company where at least 10 per cent of shares are held by a charitable foundation.

The percentage can be higher than that but not lower. The feeling among my peers is that a 10 per cent shareholding is indisputably a serious and significant shareholding in any business. The added advantage is that you can tell your colleagues that they work a half-day a week for charity.

PhilCos are sometimes described as 'foundation companies' but I prefer the shorthand of PhilCo as it can more easily be used as an identifying status in a similar vein to B-Corps. It also aligns with PhilTech, standing for Philanthropy Technology, which is the bedrock upon which Big Give's match-funding platform is built. PhilCo and PhilTech go together in ways that have the potential to be hugely impactful. There are also Steward Companies, but this is a wider category that includes employee-owned companies such as John Lewis as well as co-operatives and building societies that are built on membership models. There's nothing wrong with that; it's just that they're not PhilCos. Nor are B-Corps or companies that give away a percentage of their profits to charity every year, noble though that is. A PhilCo is defined by the charity shareholding as it's the shareholding that changes the company's DNA.

There are some very famous world-leading companies that have PhilCo status. PhilCos such as Bosch, Carlsberg, IKEA, Lego and Rolex are all linked by the fact that they are established, long-lasting brands. Each has a charitable foundation that owns a considerable portion of shares and each has a formidable reputation in their chosen markets. What's more, their reach goes way beyond their chosen markets because of the work of the associated foundation. In our case at Reed, our PhilCo has achieved so much over the last 40 years that I'm surprised, and even a little disappointed, that more business owners have not followed in a similar direction. It is my goal to inspire a whole new generation of PhilCos, better still a whole new world of PhilCos. Project PhilCo is about changing the DNA of the typical corporation and, by doing so, changing the DNA of capitalism.

Why do we need to change the DNA of capitalism? After

all, free-market capitalism has been a success story in many ways. It has lifted millions out of poverty, fuelled innovation and given people of all backgrounds the opportunity to succeed. Yet, over the last century, and certainly over the past four decades, capitalism has badly lost its way. Today shareholders wield all the power: they can buy, sell or dismantle a company as they see fit. Little thought is given to any other stakeholder, from employees to customers, let alone the wider world. We're all worse off because of it.

Supposedly rich nations are experiencing breathtakingly high levels of poverty. The relentless pursuit of profit, prioritising short-term gains over long-term value, has destroyed countless businesses that were once perfectly viable, taking with it the livelihood of unknown numbers of workers and their families. It has also led to chronic underinvestment in essential services, which has had an impact on everything from healthcare to the environment. This, in turn, has put pressure on the charity sector, with 86 per cent of charities in England and Wales reporting an increase in demand for their services, and fewer than 38 per cent confident they can meet that demand.

A reform of capitalism is long overdue. We need to make sure the model that comes next focuses on society and its needs. I call this Karma Capitalism, and I believe it has the potential to change the world and make it a better place for everyone.

The PhilCo movement is at the heart of Karma Capitalism and I have made it my life's work to make PhilCo *the* business structure of tomorrow. It is my mission to change the DNA of business. This works in every way. Embedding philanthropy into the company structure is not just about increasing the amount of money that goes to compelling causes (even though they are in desperate need, particularly since the pandemic and the cost-of-living crisis, which has decimated

OUR CO-MEMBERS ARE WORKING FOR CHARITY ONE DAY A WEEK

donations). No, being a PhilCo makes huge sense as a business strategy. Some of the world's biggest and most established and successful companies have adopted this model. Tellingly, the 40-year survival rate for PhilCos is 30 per cent, whereas for other businesses it's just 10 per cent.

What makes the PhilCo a more effective business structure? It starts with how the team feels about working for it. Our mantra has long been that with 18 per cent of the company owned by the Reed Foundation, our co-members (as my colleagues are known) are working for charity one day a week. This business model makes people more motivated, more likely to stay with us and less inclined to take sick days. While we've always sought to be a destination employer, offering attractive pay and benefits, one of the main reasons to join Reed is our work with charities.

It comes up when our co-members respond to surveys. Here are some typical comments:

*'To work for a company who would put their hands
in their pocket and donate in this way makes
me feel proud to work for Reed.'*

*'One of the main reasons I have remained working for
Reed for so long is because of the incredible charitable work
the business does which helps me to truly connect with
Reed's purpose of improving lives through work.'*

*'I have recruited many people to work for Reed during
my time and one of the unique stand-out points when
talking to candidates about joining is the charitable
work the company does.'*

Just by doing their jobs, our co-members are doing something to improve someone else's life beyond the service they

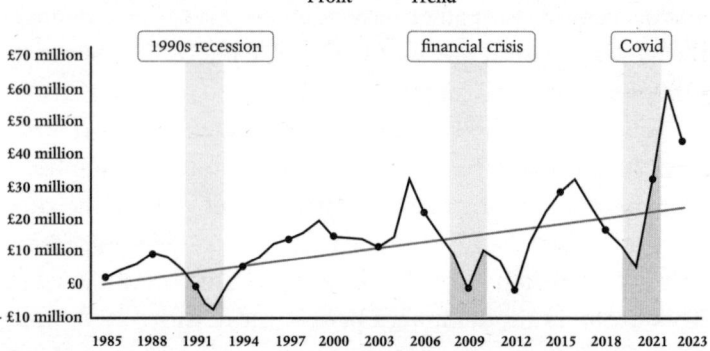

Reed's profit before tax since 1985

already provide. This is a hugely powerful message and is regularly reflected in what our co-members say about Reed. Many people join us because of it, and it has helped us do consistently well on lists of best places to work and best companies for graduates to join.

A fully engaged team translates into high performance. Here, you can see Reed's profit trajectory since the time my father first launched the Reed Foundation in 1986. (I joined the family firm not long after in 1992.) The climb in profits is steady, bar three notable dips – for the recession of the early 1990s, the global financial crisis of 2008–9 and the Covid pandemic of 2020, all events that were outside our control. The company managed to bounce back from each of those setbacks. And each time it improved its performance and increased its profits further. Again, I am convinced that this has to do with our PhilCo status and everyone on the team being fully focused on getting back on track.

This is not to forget the long list of charities we have supported over the years. The Reed Foundation has acted like a social entrepreneur, using its resources to start new charities and to invest in education. Amongst its initiatives are the successful charities Ethiopiaid and Womankind, both of which received seed funding from the Foundation. And then there are the Alec Reed Academy and the Reed Business School, both also financed in part by the Foundation. More recently, our campaign to support the victims of the Grenfell Tower fire raised £2.6 million, the biggest amount for a single campaign at that time in Reed's history. This was done through Big Give – a charity we founded in 2008 that operates a match-funding model, which means donations made by the public are doubled.

Is the world ready for Karma Capitalism? Yes and no. There will always be some fat cats who resist. Why wouldn't they? It is in their narrow interest to go on making and keeping lots of cash.

And yet I do feel that there is a groundswell of support for creating a new, more inclusive society. The younger generation in particular wants to turn its back on vulture capitalism and to feel the benefit of a more community-focused life. One of Reed's graduate recruits put it bluntly: 'My generation wants to improve on the pretty dire record of the previous one.'

The reason for writing this book is to share my thinking on how more businesses can follow this lead, become PhilCos, move towards Karma Capitalism and make the world a better place. The Reed Foundation has been going for 40 years now, and we've learned a lot along the way. The ethos of our Big Give charity fundraising model is very much about multiplying generosity. We do this by creating a digital marketplace that brings together philanthropy, business and literally thousands of good causes. We have learned that generosity is contagious. The way we spread the contagion is through something we call a match-funding campaign. We secure match funding from other PhilCos, family foundations, corporates and

BEING A PHILCO IS NOT A DIFFERENT WAY OF *DOING* BUSINESS. IT IS A DIFFERENT WAY OF *BEING* A BUSINESS.

wealthy individuals. Then we distribute those funds to charities based on how much they're able to raise from their own
supporters through their own campaigns. In a match-funding
campaign, donations are doubled. And when donations are
doubled, people give more and they give more often.

In our case, the model evolved to become what it is today.
Some of that happens by accident – one thing leads to another,
which leads to another, and then it reaches a point that no one
really expected. That was the path Reed took in its evolution
into a PhilCo, a sequence of events that led to where we are
now. I now want to use this knowledge to help the next generation focus on the most effective strategies, so that they can
make the maximum impact in the shortest space of time.

While the idea of becoming a PhilCo might seem a big
leap for any business, it is important to stress that no changes
are required from the main business model. Being a PhilCo is
not a different way of *doing* business. It is a different way of
being a business.

It changes the DNA of the business but does not need to
change what the business does from day to day. A PhilCo is all
to do with the shareholding. While I can say we work one day
a week for charity thanks to the Reed Foundation's 18 per cent
shareholding in Reed, it doesn't mean we do anything vastly
different on that day. You'd still find me working on recruitment opportunities or exploring how the latest technology
might help in job searches. But the end result, a part of the
profit from these endeavours, will end up with the Foundation, and it will be put to work for good causes.

Since launching the PhilCo movement, I have spoken to
countless entrepreneurs and the PhilCo idea is already gain-
ing traction. What appeals to them is that, as well as helping
others, the concept builds longevity into their business. The
model is a way of securing a legacy.

For those who waver, worrying that they will somehow lose out, I point to the story of Frankel, the world's leading racehorse in the early 2010s. Described as the equine Usain Bolt and rated the greatest racehorse of all time by Timeform, Frankel went through his career unbeaten. His fourteenth win out of fourteen came in the Champion Stakes at Ascot on 20 October 2012, a race I saw myself.

Our youngest daughter Taba was nine years old at the time and already in love with Frankel. She ran straight to the rails to make sure she didn't miss a moment. Frankel didn't start the race well. He almost fell out of the stalls and seemed half asleep. But after his worryingly slow start, Frankel seemed to realise where he was, moved up a gear or two and unforgettably romped home in front of a sellout crowd by one and three-quarter lengths. Knowing that I had witnessed history being made, I asked the woman behind the counter at the Tote if I could keep my betting slip. Unusually she said yes. I still have it.

This was his last race. When he retired in 2012, Frankel was valued at over £100 million. He commanded a stud fee of £125,000 a time, which rose to £350,000 by 2024. And the reason for his phenomenal success? Much has been made of his lineage as the son of Galileo, who had won the Epsom Derby, and Kind, who had won six trophies. But there are hundreds of racehorses with pedigree. The thing that made Frankel stand out, the thing the trainers and jockeys talked about, was his exceptionally big heart. When you have that, you can be more successful, do better things and make a bigger difference.

PART TWO
THE BURNING PLATFORM: CAPITALISM IN CRISIS

2
WHAT'S THE POINT OF BUSINESS?

DONATIONS ARE DOWN 17 PER CENT . . . WHILE PROFITS HAVE TREBLED

All businesses have good years and bad years. My own line of work, which is principally in recruitment and staffing services, is highly cyclical and very much reflects what is going on with the wider economy. One consequence of this is that I've learned that for a CEO, it's quite easy to run a company in a recession. You just say no all the time.

When anyone wants to spend any money, I can simply point to the downturn and say no. The opposite is also true. When things are really opening up, it's much more difficult to bat every request away. Time and resources are limited, as they always are, but when things look buoyant, decisions need to be made about how to move the company forward. Options need to be weighed and definitive choices made between this route and that.

This seemed like an eternal truth until the pandemic turned it on its head. Reed's culture already centred around what we could do for society, but when the first national lockdown hit, we redoubled our efforts to focus on sectors such as health and logistics, which really needed extra help during a dire period for jobs. As one lockdown led to another, I said no a lot less.

Our response, which included the Keep Britain Working campaign, was all about helping to preserve jobs and to redeploy those displaced from the worst-hit sectors. We also raised £5.5 million through Big Give for Covid-related charity appeals. I'm glad to say Reed was not the only company wanting to do something. In the darkest days of the pandemic, when everyone was scrutinising each other's response to the crisis, many businesses stepped forward and raised their community contributions meaningfully and noticeably.

In the post-Covid era, many a yes appears to have abruptly

switched to no. Since 2022 a lot of companies have chosen to reduce their charitable contributions as the urgency to help out seems to have largely evaporated in the face of multiple crises, both domestically and internationally. In Britain, by 2022 total donations by FTSE 100 companies had returned to the same levels as four years before the start of the pandemic, at £1.85 billion. Taking inflation into account, that represents a decline of 17 per cent in real terms. It's a similar story in the US. While the amount donated by corporates is up by a few percentage points at $36.5 billion, it has actually fallen when adjusted for inflation. And this was happening at a time when the markets were performing strongly. Despite the challenges of Covid, the FTSE 100 did well between 2016 and 2022, with total revenues rising 12 per cent from £1.54 trillion to £1.72 trillion, and total profits nearly trebling from £82.2 billion to £229.7 billion. To put this in perspective, if big business had continued to give the same proportion of pre-tax profits as in 2016, good causes would be better off to the tune of £3.74 billion.

IS SOCIAL RESPONSIBILITY BUSINESS'S RESPONSIBILITY?

Why is it that, at a time when they have become more successful, businesses have become less inclined towards philanthropy? It seems surprising, particularly in the age of instant communication and ever closer scrutiny of corporations. Yes, we all looked to business to act during the pandemic, but society still faces huge challenges on multiple fronts.

On a purely superficial level, there are a number of explanations that sound plausible. The first would be that not everyone believes it is the job of business to give lots of money to charity, or indeed any. Many corporations have followed the lead of economist Milton Friedman, who famously said: 'There is one and only one social responsibility of business – to use its resources and engage in activities designed to increase its profits.'

Writing for the *New York Times* in 1970, Friedman argued that corporate social responsibility was taking money from shareholders without authorisation or business purpose. This, he said, was bordering on fraud. Few executives are likely to be so strident these days, but there appears to be a great deal of silent support for Friedman's views.

Another reason for this reluctance to give is the potential impact on individual executives. More specifically, on their income. The decline in corporate donations as a percentage of profit has happened at the same time as the near-exponential rise in executive pay. Beyond gross salary, modern executives are now loaded up with stock options that pay out when the share price goes up above a certain point, and with other stock-related incentives. The amount they take home is thereby typically tethered to share prices, which motivates them to take short-term measures to boost the share price and with it their own bonuses. Sharing profits with charities may not seem as attractive under this arrangement. What's more, when executives are focused on short-term results, there is less time to consider philanthropy, or working towards putting any long-term measures in place to increase charitable giving.

A slightly more left-field view is that there may also be wider societal shifts at play. It seems likely that the decline in popularity of organised religion has had an impact. As a child, like most of my contemporaries, I was taken to church every week by my parents and went to a church-affiliated school. (Although, curiously, both parents have now become atheists, bucking the usual trend for people to embrace religion as they get older.) All religions emphasise hope and charity, so it was inevitable that these would be values I held in high esteem. Perhaps the reduction in church-going has also played a role in the reduced interest in charitable giving. To a generation of kids who sang 'All Things Bright and Beautiful' and went round with the collection plate, charity was part of the routine. Maybe, by losing the habit of going to church, we have also lost some of the will to give.

While each of these arguments has merit, some more than others, it seems to me that the drop in corporate giving has deeper causes. In fact, I believe it exposes flaws and vulnerabilities in the model of capitalism.

THE DANGERS OF HYPER-CAPITALISM

The concept of capitalism has undergone quite a transformation since its inception. We've gone from collaboration between people who knew one another to frequently faceless exchanges between strangers.

Arguably, capitalism in Britain began with the introduction of joint-stock companies in the Tudor era. Before then, trade was mainly conducted via guilds and liveries overseen by the elite. Each of these organisations was responsible for regulations, training, wage controls, labour conditions and standards within a particular trade, be it cloth and wool merchants, fishmongers or silversmiths.

In 1555, when Mary I was in the middle of her brief reign, the Muscovy Company became the first chartered joint-stock company. This game-changing structure allowed individuals from any background (as long as they had some cash) to pool their resources by buying shares, thus becoming shareholders in commercial ventures that spanned the globe. Joint-stock companies paved the way for non-aristocrats to financially profit from trade. In the case of the Muscovy Company, the shared goal was to find the Northeast Passage to China, but it ended up opening a lucrative trade link with Moscow, selling English wool to Russia and importing furs and other goods in return.

In the wake of the Muscovy Company's success, other joint-stock companies began to emerge. The model was simple to implement. Say, for example, a Tudor entrepreneur fancied trying his luck trading with the Far East or East Indies. If he survived the perilous journey, there would be no guarantee he could source goods of value. And, to begin with, he'd need to find a ship and an entire crew. It was all very risky and prohibitively expensive. If everything went well and he managed to bring back a ship laden with exotic goods, he would make a fortune. If not, he might lose everything.

With a joint-stock company, Tudor entrepreneurs could issue shares in their expedition. Say 100 merchants banded together to send a ship to Java. The richest merchant might put in £10 and the poorest ten shillings, but between them all, they'd get to £100. And their shareholding would reflect their contribution. The one who put in £10 would have 10 per cent, while the one who put in ten shillings would have half a per cent. This became the basis for how to set up a business.

One of the attractions of a joint-stock company was there was limited liability. If a ship sank, shareholders didn't get their money back, but the entrepreneurs who issue the shares weren't destined for the debtors' prison either. If, however, the venture was successful, the risks and rewards were distributed among a diverse group of investors, fostering a sense of camaraderie and mutual benefit. The democratisation of ownership in the following centuries was transformational, allowing the City of London to grow rapidly as capitalism developed

IT WAS ALL VERY RISKY AND PROHIBITIVELY EXPENSIVE

through the Industrial Revolution. At the same time, it also heralded a shift towards taking a sense of responsibility for the greater good. Given their proximity, the early investors in joint-stock companies – such as Cadbury, with its creation of Bournville village and its emphasis on worker welfare – were likely mindful of their impact on society, on employees and on the environment, viewing their enterprises as contributors to the wellbeing of the communities they served.

While the joint-stock concept was revolutionary in many ways, offering a wide range of people the chance to invest capital and own shares in a business, it was not a perfect model. Over time, the noble idea of shared interests and collective ownership withered and gave way to a more concentrated form of capitalism, in which the interests of a few powerful investors took precedence.

The rise of the East India Company was a case in point. The directors became so enriched by decades of trade in silks and spices that they were able to form a private army that, at its peak, numbered 260,000 men. In 1757 they used it to seize power in Bengal (today's Bangladesh) and thereafter they gained control, either directly using force or through treaties with princes, of most of what is now India and Pakistan. In the face of such vast potential riches, the original ideals of shared interests began to fade. With the concentration of power in the hands of a privileged few, concerns about economic inequality and social injustice took a back seat.

HEADS THEY WIN, TAILS YOU LOSE

Much has happened in the interim, of course, but the relentless drive towards shareholder primacy has prevailed. The focus on short-term profits often overshadows long-term sustainability and the wellbeing of the broader community. The funny thing is, from a point where companies existed to be of service to society, we all now seem to have accepted that they may not act in our best interests. There have been a few efforts to rein in the really bad actors but, on the whole, business has become very adept at resisting any sort of interference. In the last few decades, we've seen countless examples of the negative impact of this.

Consider building societies, which, in their early days, were there to help people nearby buy homes. For decades, local people would put their savings into the building society that served their district, safe in the knowledge it would be helping their children, nephews, nieces or neighbours to buy homes. These financial institutions kept money in the community and helped everyone.

When the regulations in England were loosened in the mid-1980s – under the influence of Milton Friedman – there was a rush to convert building societies into banks, owned by and accountable to shareholders. This in turn led to a spate of mergers, each one widening the gulf between the former building societies and their communities.

The deregulation of building societies was not particularly beneficial to anyone. If anything, it was the opposite. Many of these new banks sought to satisfy shareholders by expanding rapidly. This meant offering abundant credit to homeowners, which fuelled a booming housing market and a very competitive market in mortgages.

The financial crisis of 2008–9 shows how well that ended. But the impact was even worse in some specific cases. Take the Halifax Permanent Benefit Building Society, which was established in 1852 to support the community in what was then the West Riding of Yorkshire. Fast forward a century and a half and, after becoming a public company, it was merged with the

Bank of Scotland to create Halifax Bank of Scotland (HBOS), which went on to be at the centre of one of the most shocking abuses of power by any financial provider. Between 2002 and 2007, hundreds of small business customers found their accounts arbitrarily classified as 'high risk'. Their business was transferred to HBOS's Impaired Assets Division in Reading, Berkshire. Many of these business owners were forced into taking additional finance and asked to pay large fees for the pleasure. Banking executives were subsequently jailed for their role in the fraud, causing losses estimated to be more than £1 billion, but that was little comfort to the multiple businesses that went under as a result of this gigantic gulf between the needs of the company and those of its stakeholders.

The rush towards building-society deregulation highlighted another vulnerability of capitalism and the joint-stock model: it is very easy for those with an eye on the main chance to swerve in and make a pile of cash by walking away with the proceeds of the work of previous generations. In other words, asset stripping. One of the best-known examples is Enron in 2001. This is seen as an accounting scandal but, when you break it down, it is a story of executives hiding debt and inflating profits to give the illusion of success. Shareholders lost $11 billion while executives cashed in.

Every time these institutions fall, it's not just the shareholders who suffer – ordinary people lose the most. In the UK, more than 70 per cent of the once state-owned water industry is now in the hands of international investment funds, private equity and businesses registered offshore. In the years since Margaret Thatcher sold off the water companies, the industry has amassed borrowings of almost £54 billion. Not only are customers paying on average £80, or 20 per cent of their water bill, to service these debts, but there has also been a

SHAREHOLDERS LOST BILLIONS WHILE EXECUTIVES CASHED IN

noticeable drop in quality in this natural resource. And that is putting it mildly.

Nor is it just the collapse of public services that causes ordinary people to suffer. When businesses fold under the weight of debt, there can be thousands, even millions, of people impacted. This includes everyone from people who lose their jobs, and often their pensions, to suppliers and customers who are out of pocket. The financial crisis of 2008–9 saw bank bailouts total $498 billion. Who do you think paid for that? The taxpayer, of course.

The relentless pursuit of money, status and power has created a hyper-capitalist economy. For most public companies, and indeed private ones, the original ideals of joint-stock companies that were mindful of the wellbeing of society, employees and their environment are long gone. While there are a great many positives with free-market capitalism, it is simply not compatible with current requirements.

If businesses are going to step up and take their social responsibilities more seriously, something needs to change.

THE GIVING BUSINESS

In purely simplistic terms, corporations are ideally placed to play a more positive role in society because they generate wealth. In fact, there are plenty that are worth more than many states around the world. Businesses also have experience in delivering services and getting things done. A good example would be academy schools, which are run by a charitable trust independent of the local authority. If you can use commercial know-how in other areas, it can be to everyone's benefit.

We've already seen some powerful examples of successful

business leaders becoming incredible philanthropists. Warren Buffett donated more than £51 billion between 2006 and 2023 and pledged to give away almost all of the fortune he had built since 1965 with Berkshire Hathaway. Buffett was also one of the driving forces behind the Giving Pledge, a campaign whereby more than 250 ultra-rich people (including Michael Bloomberg, Larry Ellison and Mark Zuckerberg) committed to give half their wealth away to philanthropic causes.

In the entrepreneurial sector, more than 1,750 entrepreneurs across 30 countries, including Deep Mind founder Mustafa Suleyman and Kabbage COO Kathryn Petralia, have signed a legally binding agreement with the initiative Founders Pledge to donate a proportion of their personal gains to charity when they sell their businesses.

In all these cases, the sums are huge and the dedication to philanthropy admirable, but as a system it is still piecemeal. It relies on separate organisations like Giving Pledge and Founders Pledge managing to recruit a steady flow of new members to maintain momentum. The fruits of these pledges are irregular too, since Giving Pledge signatories may be around for many years to come. When it comes to Founders Pledge, the success of the initiative depends upon the entrepreneurial ventures continuing to be successful and, again, the timing is uncertain.

The wider business community needs to step up and reverse the steady decline in giving and participation. The question executives need to be asking themselves is: what is the point of business?

Many executives might follow the Milton Friedman mantra and declare that it has to make a profit. I agree with that, and our PhilCo model does not contradict it. But it's not the whole story. The world is watching. People *expect* businesses to play a responsible role in contributing to the good of wider society.

Right now, trust in business is still surprisingly high. The 2024 Edelman Trust Barometer, which measures the UK public's trust in the government, the media and business, reported an appetite for more business leadership, not less. Business, it says, is most trusted to integrate innovations into society. Of the survey group, 49 per cent trust businesses to do what is right, compared to 42 per cent for government and 35 per cent for media. This number increases when people are asked about their own employers, with 60 per cent trusting their bosses to do the right thing. The overwhelming message is that the public expects corporations to go beyond selling products and services and to support the communities in which they operate. This is, of course, an opportunity for business because any right-minded company boss would want their customers to trust them. When you order a product online, you expect to receive it. Trust is the foundation of that transaction. Customers can, and do, vote with their feet if that bond is broken. When a business picks up a reputation for being untrustworthy, it is finished.

If the carrot doesn't work, there's always the stick. In an environment of rising inequalities, growing anger and more people feeling excluded, something will eventually have to give. If no solutions are forthcoming, there will be a fragmentation between community and common purpose. Too many people feel left behind by a system that is stacked against them, leaving young people today worse off than their parents. They will be increasingly resentful of the global financial system and large corporations, seeing the benefits going only to the few. If things continue as they are, over time, this resentment of the status quo will become more widely shared. If nothing is done, there will be a total loss of confidence in our institutions and the apparent inability of business or the state to respond.

IT IS A TINDERBOX THAT COULD END UP BURNING EVERYONE

Even sustaining the status quo is impossible. The trends we see now will continue and even accelerate as people feel ever more at a disadvantage. If we do not reframe our approach, we all face a very challenging future. Such sustained harm to communities and our broader environment will further erode trust in our established institutions. This will feed into increased political uncertainty and instability. We are already seeing ample evidence of this as, according to Edelman, 'widespread grievance is eroding trust across the board . . . and the majority hold grievances against government, business and the rich'. There are plenty of real examples of culture clashes and the world seems so much more febrile than it did even a decade ago. The platform is already on fire, and it could end up burning everyone, including the asset holders.

I am not against free-market capitalism, quite the opposite. But it must be sustainable and morally supportable, and on its present course this is not the case. The only solution is for companies to become more involved in philanthropy, not less. If you believe in free-market capitalism, this is the way to keep it going.

3
THE TIME FOR ACTION IS NOW

Charities have always been at the forefront of dealing with the impacts of economic and societal shifts. We have now reached a time when many charities are so in demand that they're overwhelmed. Less than half of charitable organisations in the UK feel confident they'll be able to meet current demand and many are saying they've already reduced their services after being hit by a combination of falling income and rising costs. They are in a constant struggle to do more with less.

It won't come as a surprise that demand is rising. On the basis of land, capital and labour, the worker's share of the cake has become smaller and smaller. Employees feel like they are doing more work for less, meanwhile bosses and shareholders are getting an ever-larger slice. Inequality has soared over the past four decades in most of the advanced and major emerging economies, which together account for around two-thirds of the world's population and 85 per cent of global GDP. In the US in 2023, the ratio of a CEO's pay to that of the average worker was 192 to 1. That's not as glaring as in 2000, when it was 398 to 1. But it's still vastly greater than the 45-to-1 ratio reported in 1989, let alone the 15-to-1 ratio of 1965. The gulf between the haves and have nots is only going to get worse too. Wealth inequality is typically much higher than income inequality and feeds future income inequality through capital income and inheritance. Manufacturers of mega-yachts are unlikely to suffer any time soon, since inequality is particularly acute at the top end of income distribution – the top 10 per cent and especially the top 1 per cent. Meanwhile, those in low- and middle-income groups have seen their income share drop, with those in the bottom half feeling the greatest impact. What is equally concerning is that we are seeing growing levels of in-work poverty. This is defined as households with at least one adult working, where the income is less than 60 per cent of the national average and not enough to meet the cost of living. Sixty-three per cent of children and working-age adults in poverty in 2022/23 lived in families where at least one adult was working part-time or more, up from 44 per cent in 1996/97. It's even getting worse for 'high work intensity families' – households where both parents were working and at least one was full-time. Seventeen per cent of children and working-age adults in poverty in 2022/23 were from high work intensity families, up from 9 per cent in 1996/97.

While work was once seen as a reliable route out of poverty, now those at the bottom of the pay scale are really struggling.

THE IMBALANCE IS ACCELERATING

The West, and indeed the whole world, is facing a rapidly ageing population and the prospect of population collapse. Thanks to advances in healthcare and improvements in our diets, the likelihood of living to 100 is now far higher. By 2050, a quarter of the population in Europe and North America could potentially be 65 or over. The UK is almost there already: in 2019, over 21 per cent of the population had already hit retirement age. Nine of the ten largest economies in the world, representing 88.5 per cent of global GDP between them, need to find a way of defusing this ticking timebomb. (India is the only outlier – representing 3 per cent of global GDP.) With more and more of us living longer, there are grave implications for healthcare provision and social care, which we already know cannot be met solely by the state. Indeed, there is even less chance of meaningful state intervention, since governments need to resolve sharply rising pension costs.

There is another side to this looming threat too. The uneven balance between the old and young will put pressure

The Laffer Curve

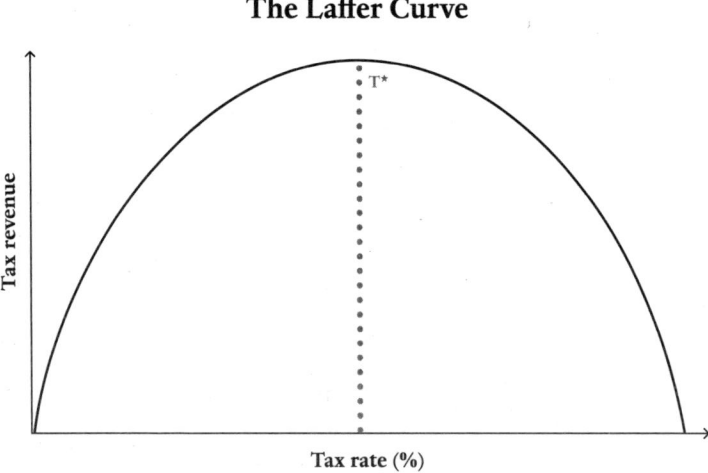

on the tax system because there will be fewer people of working age to support the ballooning older population. In this context, there is a temptation to hike taxes to pay for it. Yet there is only so far this approach can be pushed.

Just look at the Laffer Curve, the D shape that displays the relationship between tax rates and tax revenues.

The curve shows that tax revenue does not necessarily increase when the tax rate increases. If the income tax rate is set at 0 per cent, the government will receive zero revenue, but if the rate is 100 per cent, it won't receive any revenue either because there will be no motivation for anyone to go out to work.

If the tax burden increases too far and too fast, say taking away the product of half of their efforts, people will move to work elsewhere. If tax rates remain largely the same, the D of the Laffer Curve will shrink as more of the population reaches retirement, meaning less revenue and even less to spend on public services.

WHATEVER HAPPENS, STATE SUPPORT WILL INEVITABLY DROP

Whatever else happens in the future, with a declining working population, state support will inevitably drop.

Many people are fearful, and rightly so. They are fearful for their future and that of their children, fearful of the impact of the cost-of-living crisis, fearful of what might happen with the climate and environment. They need support, but there is no obvious place to turn. It is hard not to believe that the younger generation in particular have things pretty bad right now. They are worse off than their parents and can't afford to buy a home. This might be our last chance to put this right.

STORIES FROM THE SHARP END

Cardboard Citizens

Cardboard Citizens is a UK-based charity that focuses on changing the lives of homeless people through the performing arts. Founded over 25 years ago, the organisation uses theatre and art to challenge the injustices of homelessness, inequity and poverty.

When I first joined Cardboard Citizens as a Develop-ment Manager around 15 years ago, the organisation received funding from Arts Council England, together with a small handful of trusts and foundations. We had been successful in securing a recovery grant from the Arts Council that was attached to goals around diversi-fying income streams and had developed a strategy to build new relationships and support from individuals and corporate funders.

In building the case for support, we focused on helping potential funders understand why art was important for people experiencing homelessness, drawing on our long track record of experience. We were delighted to secure a relationship with a high-profile ambassador whose values and concerns reflected those of the organisation, and soon after secured support from corporate sponsors. Now we had a dynamic group who understood our cause and wanted to work with us to bring further support. At this point we decided to introduce biannual galas and began to build our network of individual donors.

The gala format worked because, for many of the individuals and corporates that we work with, the type of theatre that we make is some distance from their world. Through these carefully curated events we cre-ated a meeting point where donors and potential donors could come and see close-up how we work with people experiencing homelessness and poverty. The event would be enriched with live performances, often fea-turing large numbers of people from our membership. The galas were unique and quirky, which made all the hard work fun to be part of. The impact of these galas cannot be underestimated, helping us build up reserves that we'd never had previously.

In 2020, when Covid-19 hit, we were just about to host another gala when it had to be cancelled. We reached out to the key people who had supported us from the very start of the roll-out of our gala initiative, raised our concerns about the financial impact on the organisation and shared ideas around how to bolster support at this critical time. They immediately took up the challenge and helped run our emergency appeal. We raised enough money to pay for our core costs that year within two weeks. It was a remarkable situation to be in and something we will always be grateful for.

Our membership – comprised of people experiencing homelessness and poverty – was particularly negatively impacted by the pandemic, so we worked swiftly to refocus our programming to deliver it in a different way online. Because we were quick off the mark, we were then in a position to access additional emergency funds – because we knew we needed to offer our members additional support during that difficult period. We could be less focused on surviving and more focused on how we could evolve our offer to best meet the needs of our communities. More recently we have phased out our gala events, replacing them with the Big Give fundraising appeal, which we have found effective in attracting new support year on year. In addition, we work closely with our key supporters and board on organisational sustainability and resilience.

Lisa Briscoe, joint chief executive

ENTER THE STATE . . . OR NOT

The obvious retort we often hear is that the government needs to do more. Although public expenditure in the UK has gone up in real terms since 1997, many resources have been pared back to the bone (perhaps because so much has been wasted). Throughout the world, some of the biggest cuts in state funding were made in the aftermath of the financial crisis. In the UK, for example, the coalition government elected in 2010 introduced an austerity programme which reduced funding to local authorities and cut spending on a range of community services, including social services. What is interesting is that the then prime minister David Cameron simultaneously introduced the idea of the Big Society, a vision whereby individuals and charities would step in and fill the void. Although it was not quite billed that way. It was sold as being about 'liberation – the biggest, most dramatic redistribution of power from elites in Whitehall to the man and woman on the street'.

Despite a very different macroeconomic backdrop to today, with low inflation and higher unemployment, the Big Society failed to materialise. A later study found little evidence that cutting public-sector spending increased philanthropic activities. And the cuts have continued. In March 2023, one think tank estimated there were £21.6 billion of 'stealth cuts' to public services to come over the next five years.

Tune into any current affairs show or scroll through social media and you'll find calls for the government to do more. *We need more money. The state needs to step up.* But the government cannot afford to pick up the tab for everything. Nor does it have the competence to solve every problem. What would those same commentators say if taxes were raised by 10, 20 or even 30 per cent to pay for what some say needs to be done? It

STORIES FROM THE SHARP END

Reach Learning Disability

Reach Learning Disability is a charity based in Nottinghamshire, UK, dedicated to supporting people with learning disabilities. It offers a range of services including courses, social activities, holidays and best-practice projects. It also provides high-quality one-to-one care support.

Reach Learning Disability is a Nottingham-based charity that has been growing steadily for about 10 years. We're the largest independent charity by far dealing with people with learning disabilities. We are growing at such a rate thanks to our entrepreneurial delivery and all-encompassing service. With that growth, unfortunately, comes a bit of kickback. We've seen a drop in donations, particularly over the last 12 months, because we were seen by some funders as not needing support. Or, certainly not as much as some of the smaller charities. That is true in a way, but in another way it is not, because our *impact* is growing enormously. If we were a business, investors would be saying they wanted to invest in the one that's growing, that is getting more and more customers and satisfying more and more demand . . . whereas we're encountering a lot of nos. People want to help food banks, or those living hand-to-mouth. These are legitimate causes, but we are doing great work too.

We reciprocate where possible to any corporate who's working with us, to get them to buy into the need. We invite them to come and see us and work on one of our sites on a CSR (Corporate Social Responsibility) day. We've had quite good success in building up those partnerships, which means that we don't just become a charity of the year for one year. We work on building a much longer relationship with organisations. If you can grow the foundation model, you will find quite a lot of corporates looking to make these kind of partnerships.

Stephen Shatwell, chief executive

is fairly certain that there would be mass protests and any government that introduced such a tax regime would be quickly voted out. The conundrum is that while many people want more money to be spent on public services, few want to give up more of their own. And millions cannot afford to either.

WHEN THE STATE CANNOT STEP IN

In the clamour for more state intervention, few stop to think about the scale of the challenge. The scope of what needs to

TO DEMAND MORE OF THE STATE SEEMS LIKE AN IMPOSSIBLE AND ENTIRELY IMPRACTICAL ASK

be done is so broad, it is impossible to ask the state to cover it entirely. This was something I reflected on during a recent Big Give appeal. At the time we had just concluded a week-long appeal for charities that supported women and girls. There were around 135 beneficiaries, all doing important work, but each was different from the next, with a need that was just as pressing.

Is the state even equipped to take on a greater burden? It's difficult enough to run a company employing a workforce of 5,000 people full-time and 20,000 temporary workers, as I do. Now, scale that up to a state-run organisation that employs hundreds of thousands, perhaps more than a million people. Running a show like that must be one of the toughest jobs in the world. To demand that more requirements are dumped on the state is asking the impossible. How would it work? Surely it would be in everyone's best interests to create another environment where smaller, more nimble organisations can come to the aid of those who need it.

Some will see this as a failure of the state, because its role is to look after its people, or even a failure of democracy. And it might be. But, while any government has to be responsible and held accountable, increasing state aid is seldom a realistic option. This philosophy is out of date when it comes to the complexities of the modern world and the scale of the population. It may have been the case 100 years ago, but things have changed.

This leaves a substantial unfilled gap for another stakeholder to step forward and step up. It needs to be one with money. The obvious candidate is the business community because it has the cash and creates plenty more. What, then, if the business community says it is already doing more than enough *and* has the paperwork to prove it?

4
THE ESG DELUSION

One of my pet hates is scrolling through page after page of a company's Annual Report. It is not because I'm not interested in the detail. I most certainly am. It is just that these days you have to read through dozens, sometimes hundreds, of pages before you get to the actual numbers – the bit I want to look at (and also the point of an Annual Report). Many of these preliminary pages are filled with story after story about the company's Environmental, Social and Governance activity, or ESG, as it is better known. *Look at all the great things this company is doing!*

Granted, it is not a good look for a business to gain a reputation for the single-minded pursuit of shareholder value, with little thought for its impact on the wider world. Investors and customers expect businesses to show a sense of responsibility to the communities they operate within. This appears to be one of the reasons why businesses have wholeheartedly embraced the idea of ESG. Many are now falling over themselves to trumpet a wide range of initiatives to show they are, in fact, contributing to societal goals, through community development, ethical practices, charitable acts and environmentally responsible behaviour. The problem is that this frequently becomes a box-ticking exercise that can stray into unconvincing virtue signalling.

ESG was first mentioned in the United Nations' 2004 report *Who Cares Wins*, which formed the basis for the launch of the Principles for Responsible Investment (PRI). Here, ESG criteria were, for the first time, a requirement in the financial evaluations of companies, with the goal of encouraging businesses to develop sustainable and socially responsible investments. The idea was to create a framework that could define and measure corporate responsibility, building it around:

Environmental – including criteria such as greenhouse gas emissions, energy use and waste generation.

Social – covering fair labour practices, diversity and human rights.

Governance – involving corporate conduct and policies such as anti-corruption efforts, board diversity and executive pay.

The corporate community was quick to embrace this idea, using the framework to show their commitment to sustainability and responsible business practices. A great deal of this has been driven by big investors, who have made it clear they expect the companies they hold shares in to live up to the ESG criteria.

In the light of what we know about the decline in charitable giving by business, I wanted to know if this can be correlated with the growth in ESG. Are a corporation's good intentions now all wrapped up in their ESG agenda and is this at the expense of doing good work elsewhere?

To get to the bottom of things, I did a little number-crunching.

THE EXPLOSION IN ESG INITIATIVES

My starting point was to delve into the 2022 Annual Reports of the companies listed in the FTSE 100. I wanted to see how much space is devoted to reporting on ESG initiatives in relation to how much is spent talking about the companies' core activities and financial performance. It is a crude measure, I know, but the results are quite revealing.

On average, the income statement (profit and loss account) does not appear until page 168 of the FTSE 100 Annual Reports we examined for 2022. (About two-thirds of these 100 companies

Page no. of income statement

Barclays	p. 416
Standard Chartered	p. 340
HSBC	p. 324
NatWest Group	p. 299
Prudential plc	p. 283
Burberry	p. 265
Shell plc	p. 238
United Utilities	p. 232
Admiral Group	p. 226
Fresnillo plc	p. 226

p. = page no.

did include a summary of the income statement in their Chief Financial Officer's Report, but even this doesn't appear on average until page 49.) And some of the companies go way beyond page 168. The phrase 'written by one, read by no one' comes to mind. So what are they filling all those pages with?

Of the non-Financial Statements part of these Annual Reports, 55 per cent on average is devoted to ESG. Most of that (39 per cent) goes on Governance, with 9 per cent on Environmental and 7 per cent on Social. These sections usually feature before the Financial Statements, with the Governance section coming just before them.

Governance typically includes profiles of the board and reports from the Nomination, Audit and Remuneration Committees (and any other board committees).

Environmental and Social are often grouped together under Sustainability and sometimes linked explicitly to the UN Sustainable Development Goals from 2015.

- The Environmental section includes Task Force on Climate-related Financial Disclosures, which the UK has made mandatory from April 2022 for all companies that have more than 500 employees and are banks or insurance companies, have publicly traded shares or have turnover above £500m.

- Some companies have also included the EU Taxonomy for sustainable activities, a framework for classifying which economic activities are environmentally sustainable. This was introduced in 2020 and is currently voluntary in the EU. The UK is developing its own taxonomy.

By comparison, other elements of the Annual Report include:

- Analysis of risks facing the company and a Viability Statement (stating that the directors have assessed the longer-term viability of the company – an obligation introduced in 2014). This is 9 per cent of the content on average, although the figure is much higher for banks.

- Details of how the company engages with stakeholders, including an S172 Statement, referring to Section 172 of the Companies Act 2006, which states that the directors have a duty to 'promote the success of the company . . . for the benefit of its members as a

whole', meaning all stakeholders. Average proportion
of content: 3 per cent.

- The Financial Report: analysis of the financial performance of the company, including income, costs,
profit, balance sheet, cash flow and so on. Average
content: 6 per cent.

- The Auditors' Report is the one bit of the whole thing
that is not the responsibility of the directors. While this
takes up 11 pages on average, the information could
be contained on a single page. Nearly everyone who
peruses accounts is simply interested in whether the
company is a going concern and its accounts give a
'true and fair view', whether they comply with the
Companies Act and appropriate accounting standards,
and whether there are any material uncertainties that
the auditors need to draw the reader's attention to.
Average content: 7 per cent.

- Finally, there is the Strategic Report, which much of
the above technically falls into. It includes the rest of
the non-financial statements, such as the Chairman's
Report and Chief Executive's Report, and a discussion
of the performance of different divisions of the company, strategic initiatives, new products, services or
systems. Average content: 20 per cent.

You may be wondering about Reed's own Annual Report.
Well, I am acutely aware that it too has seen a rise in the
amount of ESG reporting. I am someone who firmly believes
in keeping things simple, and my preference is always to avoid
unnecessary copy, but there is a certain amount of this information we must now include. However, looking back over the
past 15 years, had we been in the FTSE 100, we would have been
in little danger of troubling the top ten. Here are the details:

Page no. of income statement

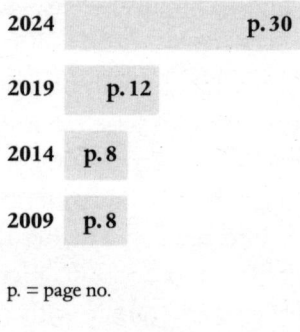

2024	p. 30
2019	p. 12
2014	p. 8
2009	p. 8

p. = page no.

Reed Global page no. of income statement increases over time (2009 vs 2024)

— Trend — page no.

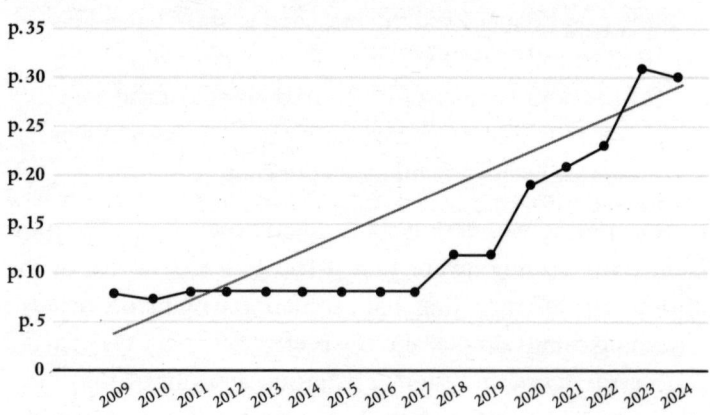

p. = page no.

SMOKE AND MIRRORS

While these statistics are undeniably a crude measure, they do show that the attention paid to ESG vastly outweighs the rest of the information in the report, even the numbers. But it is when you dig into the detail beneath the surface that the alarm bells really begin to ring.

While I am not against the goals of ESG, because, as a concept, it is broadly right, my instinct is that many of these initiatives have become meaningless virtue signalling, or box-ticking exercises. Anecdotal evidence from members of my Reed team bears this out. When we pitch for jobs, we are frequently asked by prospective clients to fill out lengthy questionnaires about our ESG initiatives and what actions we will be taking alongside the contract in question. Very often this will also require signing up to become accredited on one of the many new online services being built to serve the burgeoning ESG industry, paying anything from £4,000 to £20,000 for the pleasure. Here's the thing though. After we have won a contract, it is exceedingly rare for ESG promises to be mentioned at all. In the words of one of my team: 'Unless someone at the client organisation is super-keen on ESG, no one really holds you to the promises made.'

Does this make a difference? To our clients or our customers? I would argue it does. Because when the proposed initiatives are just words, some businesses will say anything to win a contract. What we see is an escalation of promises. It's as if you or I had pledged to score 50 goals a season for Liverpool. If that was taken at face value, as many ESG pledges are, one of us would have been signed over Mo Salah and millions of fans would have been very disappointed.

The problem is that it's not just empty promises that are at issue here. There are a whole lot more question marks hanging over ESG. Here are five of them:

1 Lack of regulation and standardisation

There are few regulations, standardised metrics and reporting frameworks around ESG claims. This makes it nigh on impossible to accurately, or consistently, compare and evaluate a company's sustainability performance. In the UK, for example, ESG policy comes under a combination of domestic and EU-derived laws and regulations. Not all companies are subject to the regulations and those that are are subject to a mix of voluntary disclosures and mandatory reporting requirements.

This lack of uniformity can lead to inconsistencies and confusion among stakeholders about the significance of ESG claims. It also opens the way for corporations to embellish or overstate their efforts.

2 Incomplete or selective reporting

Companies may selectively report positive aspects of their sustainability efforts while ignoring or downplaying negative impacts of their day-to-day operations, creating a misleading perception of their overall sustainability performance. To understand how this might happen, it is worth noting that in the FTSE 100, the list of the ten top-rated companies for ESG includes one of the world's most prolific plastic polluters, two coal and gas giants, two mining groups and a tobacco company. Laudable though their ESG efforts may be, questions must surely be asked whether their overall impact on the planet is not still negative.

3 Insufficient integration into core business practices

Many companies treat ESG initiatives as entirely separate from their core business strategies. Surely, to be truly effective, ESG initiatives should be fully integrated into a company's culture, operations and decision-making processes, instead of being somehow disconnected.

I am reminded here of the Harvard academic and business consultant Clayton Christensen, who wrote that the purpose of companies is to focus on jobs that need to be done. Thus, a car manufacturer like Toyota makes cars and a recruitment company like Reed is there to find new hires for its clients.

Grandstanding that 'we're all about sustainability' or 'we have ambitious climate targets' and then planting some trees, rather than getting on with making the main business cleaner, more efficient and sustainable, just doesn't sit right with me. It is not entirely honest either. There is also a question mark about whether or not it is in the interests of the stakeholders to lose sight of the core purpose of the business. Barclays Bank's Annual Report takes over 400 pages to reach the financial statements but in recent times it has closed hundreds of branches. No doubt many of its customers are concerned about ESG, but I'd bet that more of them might like to see a bank in their neighbourhood. ESG can be a bureaucratic distraction too. Time spent on certain initiatives means a team may well offer a poorer service to their customers, because there is less time to deliver the goods or services that businesses are paid to deliver.

4 Lack of accountability

Change only counts if it's real and, often, companies are not as sustainable as they claim to be. Yet there is little in the way of independent verification or third-party audits, making any company's ESG claims difficult to authenticate.

This lack of accountability will, in the long term, lead to scepticism and cynicism, undermining the credibility of ESG initiatives. Even now, though, do we know how much more included and involved people feel? How do we know that funds allocated to social causes are delivering an improvement to the lives of the communities they are allegedly spent on? (And by what metric should this be measured?) When businesses claim to have worked with a supplier to offset *x* amount of carbon by planting *xx* number of trees, is this really happening? One survey into the burgeoning \$2 billion (£1.46 billion at the time of writing) voluntary-offsets market found that more than 90 per cent of rainforest offset credits are more likely than not phantom credits. They do not represent genuine reductions at all. We might feel better when we're told that the products we buy are carbon-neutral, or that we can eat certain foods without adding to the destruction of the planet, but the reality might not be so clear-cut.

5 Lack of immediacy

It is not just the substance of ESG targets that is woolly. The timing is too. Take climate change as a case in point. Many companies make much of their focus to meet UN goals to reach net zero by 2050, as set out in the Paris Agreement. But, while most would agree that we need initiatives to address climate change, the net zero targets are just too easy to evade, or to kick into the long grass.

I CAN'T HELP WONDERING WHAT OUR GRANDCHILDREN WILL SAY

Most of the people who signed up to being net zero in 2050 (including executives who see to it that these pledges are reiterated in their Annual Reports) won't be alive by 2050. I *hope* we reach net zero by 2050, but it all feels a little far off and a little meaningless to me. I can't help wondering what our grandchildren and great-grandchildren will say. I doubt it will be 'they really nailed it'. If ESG is mentioned at all, it will more likely be 'what a joke'.

If you think about sustainability in terms of running a corporation, the two aims are not readily compatible. Businesses think in days and months. CEOs ask, 'What can I do to grow this business today?' The fact that ESG targets are so often far in the future is a giveaway, showing that they are not quite as prominent as everyone is claiming.

The biggest issue with ESG is not just that it can be so easily manipulated. It is that it is *purposefully* misleading. It has become increasingly profitable for companies to be seen as green to encourage investments and funding, rather than making more genuine commitments.

GOOD DEEDS OR A LOAD OF OLD GREENWASH?

You will have heard of sportswashing, whereby individuals, corporations and, these days, entire nations use the halo of high-profile sports events to make them look better. Let me introduce you to green, blue, pink and social washing – the entire portfolio of terms that have emerged to describe false or misleading claims about ESG credentials.

Greenwashing

Greenwashing has roots going back to the 1980s when, as concern began to grow about what we are doing to our planet, businesses saw an opportunity to burnish their eco-credentials by creating a misleading impression that their products or services are environmentally friendly. The fact that businesses associated with hydrocarbons, tobacco and chemicals often appear to shout the loudest about this tells us quite a lot. It's no coincidence that companies in these sectors favour logos that are yellow and green, suggesting sunshine and landscape. This can be an obvious attempt to shift attention from a poor environmental record.

Bluewashing

This concerns the UN Global Compact, a framework centring around ten principles in the areas of human rights, labour, the environment and anti-corruption. Announced with great fanfare at the 1999 World Economic Forum, the Global Compact now boasts 17,000 participants from over 160 countries. Its major flaw is that it is not a legally binding framework. Corporations can make PR capital out of their association with the UN's efforts at creating a better world, but there is no mechanism or oversight to make sure the principles are properly followed. Commentators have called the initiative 'meek' and accused many of the signatories with questionable records in adhering to environmental law or human rights of 'hypocrisy'.

Pinkwashing

Every June, the Internet and social media fill with rainbow-coloured corporate logos. Companies all over the world, even those that are usually sticklers for strict brand identity guidelines, allow their logos to be switched for Pride month, signalling their commitment to the LGBTQ+ community. The question that is not asked frequently enough is: what are these businesses doing for the other 11 months of the year to make sure their LGBTQ+ colleagues feel safe and included (or, indeed, during Pride month itself, other than changing logos)? More than half of LGBTQ+ people in a 2022 survey in the US reported experiencing some sort of workplace discrimination or harassment, and that number jumps to 70 per cent for transgender respondents. A cynic might say it costs next to nothing to change your logo for a short period. It is just symbolism. Meaningful change requires investment – in money, time and commitment.

Whitewashing

Social washing is a catch-all term that neatly summarises much of the above, but I'd rather just call it whitewashing, which is what all of this really is. Essentially, organisations are marketing themselves as socially conscious and supporting the big issues of the day, but the reality is nowhere near as clear-cut. Far from it, in fact. While many firms do actively consider the rights of employees and stakeholders, many do not and simply say they are addressing worker rights/examples of discrimination/environmental issues/sustainability (delete as appropriate). It is very easy to make a lot of noise but, when it comes to the substance of the claims, it is all too readily taken as a given.

I suppose some might ask what is the problem with a bit of whitewashing, or indeed any colour of washing? After all, any company will want to look its best and present a positive brand identity – that's why they spend a fortune on marketing. The most obvious danger is when a little bit of puffery turns into downright dishonesty, misleading customers and the wider population. Volkswagen's six-year 'Clean Diesel' campaign, which ran until 2015, is a good example. The idea was to disprove the notion that diesel emitted more airborne pollutants than unleaded fuel. When Volkswagen was exposed for rigging 11 million of its diesel cars with emission-cheating software, it was revealed that diesel emitted *40 times* the legally permitted level of nitrogen dioxide. In 2020 the company announced that the deception had cost it €31.3 billion (£26.8 billion) in fines and settlements.

That's not to say that all companies are trying to be deliberately misleading or have bad intentions. However, what it does add up to is the same thing: a lack of transparency with consumers, stakeholders and investors, and misleading language being used to market a given product or service as more sustainable than it really is. Over time, these exaggerated claims erode trust. Meanwhile, there is no meaningful change – which is surely the whole point of ESG.

ESG ECLIPSES CHARITABLE GIVING

Whichever way you look at it, ESG is monopolising businesses, Annual Reports and the tendering process. Right now, there is no change in sight. If you do not play the game, you won't get the business. There will come a point where it becomes widely recognised that we've created a meaningless ESG industry in which no one is really better off. Or that while the intentions were good, ESG has been diverted from its main purpose.

While I am not disputing the objectives, I am disputing the process. The suspicion is that this bandwagon may have a bit of time to run yet. I can be critical of ESG because I run a privately owned company and do not need to answer to the markets. There is currently a lot of pressure from investors for publicly quoted firms to comply, so it would take a brave CEO of any listed company to stand up and question whether this is all really working as it should be.

While I hate to see wasted time and money, and find ESG an irritating distraction, my biggest complaint about things as they stand is that ESG can make organisations hugely selective, single-minded and even insular in the causes they support. Fashionable causes come and go. This year it might be carbon capture, next year the elimination of plastics. Again, worthy causes. But, in the scramble to make commitments to whatever it is that is mostly being talked about online and in the media, many, many other worthwhile initiatives will be overlooked.

It is not a huge leap in logic to say that the marked drop in charitable giving and engagement amongst corporations is most likely linked to the rise in ESG. This is where the energy is now being directed and it is to the detriment of less high-profile, yet nevertheless important, causes. Although charitable initiatives are often flagged up in the Environmental or Social sections of Annual Reports, which shows that at least some attention is being directed towards this area, even this can be slightly misleading. Very often, activities that are flagged as charitable do not involve a registered charity, whether one set up by the business or an independent company. Things included in these sections frequently trumpet that the company is reducing its carbon footprint,

WE NEED A DIFFERENT KIND OF CAPITALISM

or waste generally, or it is supporting LGBTQ+, disabled, ethnic-minority or female employees, or encouraging staff development. Though this is good to hear, none of these activities involve what you would traditionally deem to be a charity.

From a purely personal viewpoint, as the CEO of a large business, I find it frustrating how much time is spent on ESG in our organisation. I know for a fact we can make much more of an impact by putting our weight behind our PhilCo status, which helps us to raise tens of millions of pounds for charities every year, rather than by expending multiple working hours making sure our office fridges are compliant. Don't get me wrong. I can definitely see the upside of making sure the lights are turned off when the office is empty, or of turning the heating down. (Apart from anything else, it saves the business money.) But I am much more interested in meaningful initiatives that make a real difference to people and to organisations that might not otherwise receive any funding at all.

My criticism of the current ESG regime doesn't mean I am advocating for new rules. Far from it. There has been an accumulation of regulations going back about 30 years, and businesses are already buckling under the growing weight of bureaucracy. Nor do I want to advocate for a costly review. There has been enough money wasted on this already.

No, we need our corporations to have the freedom to be productive, so that they can keep delivering the goods and services that society wants. Imposing more and more rules makes it more and more difficult for them to be so. What I am arguing for goes far beyond this. We need to completely rethink the model so businesses can focus more on actions – the right actions – rather than words.

We need a different kind of capitalism: a new variant of it, one that aligns the interests of business and society to make a meaningful difference. Let some of the profits be allocated to good causes, which genuinely improve our environment and social outlook, contributing to specific, verified and measurable outcomes.

PART THREE
THE CASE FOR REAL CHANGE

5
IN SEARCH OF . . . LONGEVITY

If you were to walk into the office of pretty much any chief executive of a certain vintage, there are three well-thumbed books you would be almost certain to find on their shelves: *In Search of Excellence* by Tom Peters and Robert H. Waterman Jr and *Built to Last* and *Good to Great* by Jim Collins (the former with Jerry Porras).

People don't write business books like these any more. This trio of bestsellers share a common topic – how to create an enduringly successful business. Between them, they cite 50 of the most widely admired businesses of the time. It is safe to assume that at least part of the popularity of these books is down to the fact that most businesses do not survive very long.

When it comes to long-term success, nothing is a given. Even the most dominant category leaders, companies that once looked rock-solid, can disappear from view. And that situation is getting worse. The average lifespan of a company on Standard and Poor's 500 index is just over 21 years today, compared with 32 years in 1965. Meanwhile, three-quarters of FTSE 100 companies (76 per cent) don't reach their twenty-first birthday.

What I find interesting about these books is that many of the companies held up as exemplars of how to succeed and create a business for the long term turned out to be not quite as 'excellent' or 'great' or 'built to last' as they were cracked up to be. Among these 50 firms, Kodak, Kmart, Circuit City and Wang filed for bankruptcy. Many businesses lost their independence after being acquired, including Amoco (bought by BP), Gillette (P&G), Raychem (Tyco International), DEC (Compaq) and Data General (EMC). As it turned out, this elite group of 50 companies were not so elite after all.

For full disclosure, I should say, I once worked with Tom Peters and hugely admire him. He is a barnstorming public speaker who gives fantastically energetic and inspirational talks to business managers. We met when I was working at the BBC, which I had joined in 1990, following my time at Harvard Business School. I had been put in charge of producing a programme called *Crazy Ways for Crazy Days*. It was a time when there was a lot of change and development in the world of business with the emergence of the Internet, mobile telephones and network computing. Our programme featured Peters, who took us through case studies of four companies including engineering firm Asea Brown Boveri (ABB) and family-owned trucking company the Lane Group. The hour-long film, which was shown on BBC Two, was then repackaged and sold around the world by BBC Enterprises as an educational programme with case studies. It sold well and grossed over £1 million.

What happened next was partly responsible for my move into Reed. On the back of the response to the Tom Peters episode, I asked my bosses at the BBC for a similar budget for a new project. Given the commercial success of the Tom Peters film, which had delivered a big return on investment, I was hoping for financial backing to do more of the same. The answer, when it came, was a firm 'no'. This rejection seemed a bit ridiculous to me and put me off remaining at the BBC. Later, when my father asked if I wanted to join him in the family business, it was one of the reasons I said 'yes'.

In his analysis of corporate longevity, Tom Peters identified eight things that were essential.

1. **A bias for action**
   To innovate and grow, businesses need to have a 'can do' approach and be prepared to try, fail, try again and keep trying until they succeed.

2. **Close to the customer**
   Yup, the customer is still important, however complex the business and however distanced the management may be from the end user.

3. **Autonomy and entrepreneurship**
   Big businesses need the nimbleness of small ones. Customers do not relate well to gigantic monoliths.

4. **Productivity through people**
   An organisation is nothing without its people. Oh, and it takes more than just talking about 'engagement' to convince teams that their employers have their backs.

5. **Hands-on, value-driven**
   Organisations need to define what they stand for and what will make their teams take pride in where they work, and then actively manage towards it.

6. **Stick to the knitting**
   Mergers with other companies to grow the business are rarely successful, especially if there is no synergy between the two entities.

7. **Simple form, lean staff**
   Keep a simple, workable and minimum staffing structure, even in a complex organisation. This can include outsourcing some activities and creating time-limited taskforces for specific projects.

8. **Simultaneous loose-tight properties**
   Combine tight management control of the fundamentals with a system that supports autonomy, innovation and entrepreneurship.

Some of these maxims may come as a surprise to contemporary business leaders, but to me they are as relevant today as ever.

Meanwhile, *Good to Great* companies are, according to Jim Collins, built on resolute yet modest leadership; first focusing on the who, then the what; disciplined thoughts; and exacting standards. *Built to Last*, on the other hand, focuses on visionary companies that are driven by core values and purpose; Big Hairy Audacious Goals (BHAGs); smooth transitions between leaders; and an appetite for change, however uncomfortable. These goals are delivered by what Collins refers to as Level 5 leaders, who are modest, dedicated to their work, and put others' needs above their own.

THE TRUE SECRET OF A LONG CORPORATE LIFE

While these books make a number of very valid points about what elements contribute to the great businesses of their day and today, they do not appear to have cracked the secret of longevity. An analysis by the management consultancy firm McKinsey found that, when it came to the companies cited in the three books, the odds of them outperforming the market were 52-48, which is not much better than the toss of a coin. As for those that have retained their place at the top, various theories have been advanced as to why. Being on the right side of major trends, like the growth in IT, or simply changes in legislation, is often enough to make the difference between success and failure. Those companies that fail to grasp the importance of these new developments fade, while those who are quick to spot an opportunity pivot, adapt and prosper.

When it comes to identifying the true secret of a long and successful corporate life, perhaps we've been going about it all wrong. We might discover a whole lot more by looking at companies that have survived for decades and analysing what they have in common.

I inadvertently did just this when looking at other businesses that have a similar PhilCo model to Reed's, combining business ownership with philanthropy (sometimes referred to elsewhere as being a 'foundation company'). Priority is given to the overall business goal, but a percentage of profits will be managed by a separately run foundation which divides its share of the profits among charitable causes. There are a few differences in structure, in that some of the companies are private, so their shares will not be publicly traded, while others are quoted, with shares bought and sold by the public on stock exchanges. However, what they do have in common is their longevity.

Let me share some interesting early details from my own research. I picked ten household-name companies that I like and admire, all with shares owned by a connected foundation, and then looked at how long they had been in existence. See what you notice from the list below:

Of the foundation companies on my list, our own company Reed, at 65 years old, is a relative adolescent when compared to the likes of Lindt and Carlsberg, both of which are closing in on their 200th birthdays. However, my own small snapshot has been backed by extensive surveys elsewhere. One study found that the probability of companies with this structure surviving more than 40 years is 30 per cent, compared with just 10 per cent for other firms.

The research made me think about my own experiences. I remember as a boy visiting Port Sunlight, the picturesque village in Merseyside near where my uncle and aunt used

Built to last: Longevity of Foundation-owned Companies

Company	Country	Company type	Years in business
ABF	UK	Public and foundation-owned	90
Bosch	Germany	Private and foundation-owned	138
Carlsberg	Denmark	Public and foundation-owned	177
IKEA	Sweden	Private and foundation-owned	81
LEGO	Denmark	Private and foundation-owned	92
Lindt	Switzerland	Public and foundation-owned	180
Maersk	Denmark	Public and foundation-owned	121
Patagonia	USA	Private and trust-owned	52
Reed	UK	Private and foundation-owned	65
Rolex	Switzerland	Private and foundation-owned	120

to live. This was built in 1888 by the 'Soap King' William Hesketh Lever, to house the workers at Lever's soap factory. George Cadbury did a similar thing, buying 120 acres near his chocolate factory in Birmingham in 1895, which became the Bournville village. We are all very familiar with these brands, which have clearly stood the test of time. Cadbury and Unilever are standout companies that have become part of our cultural as well as our commercial landscape.

It seems to me, if we are searching for the secret of corporate longevity, we should look at companies with a different DNA, and start our search among companies that have combined business ownership with philanthropy.

THE PHILCO MODEL

The reality that underpins PhilCos is these businesses are focused on more than simply short-term, profit-maximising strategies to enrich a small group of shareholders. Instead, the business becomes a force for common good, breaking down the barriers between business and philanthropy to create meaningful change for *all* stakeholders, including workers, customers, suppliers, communities and good causes. In this way, PhilCos perform a dual purpose:

- **Economic:** This is where a business acts in a way similar to all others, enacting the vision and strategy of the founder and the team at the top, to serve customers, make profits and maintain the stability of the company or, better still, grow it in the face of an ever-changing market.

- **Philanthropic:** Through the payment of dividends, a pre-determined proportion of profits are shared with charitable projects not necessarily connected to the main thrust of the business, in compliance with the share-ownership allocations prescribed at the time this structure was agreed, most commonly set down by the company founder.

Typically, the PhilCo board will be very much as you'd expect to see in any conventional business operation, with a chairman, chief executive, senior executives and non-executives on the board looking after the commercial interests of the company. The foundation is entirely separate, with a non-profit board that is unpaid and completely independent of the day-to-day operations of the company. The trustees on this board cannot be removed, or replaced, by anyone except themselves.

Their entire purpose is to further the foundation's charitable purposes for the public benefit, *not* the benefit of the business.

The PhilCo model is better known in mainland Europe, particularly in Denmark. A quarter of the 100 largest companies there have a PhilCo structure, representing 60 per cent of the country's stock market capitalisation. This type of firm was also common in the US up until 1969 and the passing of the Tax Reform Act, which strongly prohibited them. The rules were substantially amended there in 2018, but this structure is only permitted if the foundation holds 100 per cent of the voting rights of the PhilCo it is linked with. There are some notable examples in the UK, including ABF, EQ Investors, PZ Cussons and Lloyd's Register, but they are by no means common. There are a multitude of explanations for this, and I believe one of the primary ones is custom. The model is simply better known in Denmark, and so it has become the norm, whereas in markets such as the UK it is still quite unusual. There are also no tax incentives in the UK to structure a company in this way, which there are elsewhere.

Before going into the wide range of business advantages to be gained from a PhilCo structure, over and above providing *genuine* support to good causes, let's first look at why companies that have adopted it are so enduring.

A solid future by design

One of the criticisms levied at businesses, particularly publicly quoted companies, is a tendency towards short-termism. In days gone by the norm was to build a company over time, while providing a good service to customers, whereas today it is often about achieving ever-growing returns in the shortest timeframe. Corporations typically think in terms of quarters or sometimes even less, because that is what the markets demand.

There is also a focus on releasing money from the business to meet the high expectations of directors and shareholders. This often means the lifespan of a business is abruptly cut short when a halfway credible offer is made by a third party. The offer may not be in the long-term interests of the business, its customers or other stakeholders, but a bird in the hand and all that.

Nowhere is this tendency more acute than in private equity. Here, the entire financial model is based on buying businesses in the hope of flipping them for a profit a few years later. During the intervening period, a sophisticated financial box of tricks is deployed, but frequently what it all boils down to is taking all the cash in the business out and putting a lot of loans in. The borrowings do not go into investing in the business, or its people, but rather straight into releasing cash to investors. This leaves any business owned by private equity on the hook for a large amount of debt, which it has to work very hard to service.

Companies often buckle under the strain. Businesses bought out by private equity are *ten times* more likely to go bust than those that are not. We've heard countless stories of once-successful firms driven to the brink in this way, including the Morrisons supermarket group and retailers Cath Kidston and Toys 'R' Us. The damage that this can do was really brought home to me when, in February 2024, The Body Shop, a firm I know well, went into administration just weeks after being acquired by a private-equity firm.

It was The Body Shop that gave me my first proper job. Anita Roddick, its legendary founder, hired me in 1984, the year when the company went public on the London Stock Exchange after just eight years in business. Growth had been brisk because customers really bought into the message that this cosmetics company could be a force for good, supporting fair trade, not testing products on animals and doing the right thing in business. I worked closely with Anita and her

BUSINESSES BOUGHT OUT BY PRIVATE EQUITY ARE TEN TIMES MORE LIKELY TO GO BUST

husband, Gordon, on various projects both in the shops and their offices, and I learned a huge amount from them both.

Fast forward 40 years and Aurelius, a German private-equity firm, took over The Body Shop, paying £207 million for it. The price reflected the fact that the business had been going through a rocky period for a while. When it had been sold to a Brazilian cosmetics company, Natura, in 2017, the price was £880 million. In the seven intervening years, The Body Shop's value had plummeted, but as it turned out, it still had further to go. Three months after acquiring it, Aurelius announced it was unable to revive the fortunes of The Body Shop and promptly put it into administration. What really stinks is that Aurelius had been given precedence over other creditors and all the loans that it made to The Body Shop were repaid ahead of everyone else.

In an ironic twist, The Body Shop owed Reed over £100,000 for supplying them with temporary workers, which we now had little prospect of getting back. It is hard not to feel sad and slightly embittered that the story of this pioneering retailer should end like that. I joined The Body Shop as a young man, full of youthful enthusiasm and learned from these great entrepreneurs. Then, later in my career, a company I loved had come to a sad end. It had lost its soul.

Removing the vulnerability

How, then, you may be wondering, could PhilCo status help a company like The Body Shop, or any other business that attracts the attention of possible acquirers? Most businesses have a built-in vulnerability. When an offer is made, the board and shareholders will vote on it and there is always a certain amount of self-interest involved. In almost all circumstances, a sale will enrich the senior team, so it is a noble executive who sees past this and thinks instead of the long-term interests of their business. The same goes for shareholders, who, of course, tend to welcome a big pay-out.

Let's imagine that, in another life, I am a ruthless private-equity person, casting an eye over a business like Reed. Or perhaps I am running another complementary business and reckon I have spotted some synergies. In both cases, let's face it, as the predator, I am looking for a good payday. I know exactly what I would do with this recruitment business too. I would make a compelling offer, then, once I took ownership of Reed, I would take all the cash out and replace it with debt. I would also sell all its property, lease it back and pocket the money. I would pretty much be guaranteed to make a personal fortune. Sure, there is every chance that the company might not survive under its debt burden, but that wouldn't be my concern. It would be sold again, long before the company that bought it next found out.

The PhilCo model can make this type of predatory takeover much more difficult. If, say, my grandchildren decided they wanted to cash in, they might let it be known that they were open to offers. Or, certainly, they would not immediately turn away any suitors that came to the door. But *the majority* of the shareholders would need to agree that being sold was in the company's best interests. That would include our largest single shareholder, the Reed Foundation, which manages our philanthropic interests and the 18 per cent of company profits that are channelled through it. Foundation boards are largely impervious to shareholder votes and hostile acquisitions because their primary goal is to secure a good return for the charity over the long term. Yes, there is a possibility that the trustees will say this is a good deal and in the best interests of the company. It is, however, more likely they resist because it may not be in the *long-term* interests of the philanthropy side of the equation. There are, after all, no guarantees that any acquirer will want to remain a PhilCo.

One of the best-known examples of trustees resisting a take-over is the Novo Nordisk Foundation. You may well be familiar with this Danish drug company, not least because, at the time of writing, it is Europe's most valuable company, thanks to its pioneering weight-loss and diabetes drugs Wegovy and Ozempic. The foundation owns 77 per cent of Novo's voting rights and 28 per cent of its shares. A few years back, before the two wonder-drugs were launched, the directors of the main business suggested that the company might be sold, which would have easily netted several billion dollars. The trustees of the charity said no, they didn't think it was in the interest of the company to sell it because the company's long-term prospects were better served by its current structure. Since they had the bulk of the voting rights, the sale didn't go ahead. At the time, no one knew that Wegovy and Ozempic would transform the company's fortunes. Thanks to the trustees, though, the company retained its independence, and it is now one of the top three philanthropic organisations in the world by granting capacity.

The strength of the resistance to predatory takeover action is, of course, dependent on the percentage of shares allocated to and held by the charitable foundation. If the foundation holds 100 per cent of the shares, as is the case with several of the European PhilCos listed in this chapter, it will be super-resistant. But even with a smaller share held by a charitable foundation, it is harder work for another company to sweep in to make a deal. There will be easier pickings elsewhere, in companies where the shareholding is less well equipped to stand up to hostile takeovers.

The PhilCo model encourages businesses to think long term, as is demonstrated by the longevity of the companies that have adopted it. Directors of PhilCos need not fear imminent removal by shareholders or talk of a sale if things do not shape up quickly in the short term. Less backseat driving and

LESS BACK-SEAT DRIVING IS GOOD FOR LONGEVITY

more autonomy is good for longevity. There are, however, many more advantages that help build a solid foundation to support PhilCos from decade to decade.

This model also guarantees that a company's future can be self-determined. This is something Stephan Schenk discovered when he turned to this structure after a terrible experience with early backers. While Stapelstein, the brand Schenk founded in 2016, is far younger than all the businesses mentioned here, it is hoped that, as a PhilCo, it now has the ability to go the distance, something that was very much in doubt with its previous structure.

Stapelstein, which looks for ways to help children keep moving, was founded when Schenk was still at university. He devised a simple, colourful series of modular objects, with the goal of creating a wide range of incentives to get children playing, interacting and using their energy. While he was pleased to have attracted some early investment from two business angels, he quickly realised that he had made a mistake. He had traded most of his company away in the process, including the all-important voting rights.

When the business went into profit, Schenk soon discovered that he and the investors had very different visions for the future of Stapelstein. He was eager to reinvest the profits to grow the business, while they wanted to take money out via dividends. As a minority shareholder, he was not able to overrule them. To extricate himself and his company from the situation, and to protect Stapelstein's original purpose, he moved to become a PhilCo (also known as steward company), working with capital partners Purpose Ventures and Purpose Evergreen Capital. To achieve this, he had to buy out the other two shareholders. While one shareholder sold out fairly soon, it took 18 months and a lot of money to persuade the second to sell.

stapelstein®

STORIES FROM THE SHARP END

Stapelstein

Stapelstein is a company that creates versatile, open-ended play products designed to inspire children to move more and explore their creativity. Its colourful, durable foam blocks are made from eco-friendly materials.

I come from a family where there is no connection to business. We all work in social professions, such as care homes, kindergartens and schools. It is probably why I chose to create such a product. As a product designer, I connected with my personal background. I trusted the investors 100 per cent, thinking they had really connected with the idea and wanted to create this purpose-driven company together with me.

There was a moment when the trust relationship tipped in the wrong direction. The preferred option for the angels was to sell the whole company to another investor or a big toy company. It was pretty clear that there was no easy way out. It was a dilemma and a challenging time, but I learned pretty fast.

I heard about steward companies by watching a documentary about the Purpose Foundation. I contacted them to share my story and they were very supportive. They had the right tools and the funds to help me to change the model and guided me through the process of becoming a steward-owned company. There was a long journey to find the right price that my former shareholder would agree to. The negotiations were very complex, involving lawyers from the Purpose Foundation network. The shareholder could have easily said no. We could not force him to sell, yet we depended on his decision. He did eventually agree, leaving me finally able to focus on the purpose of Stapelstein.

By far the most important thing to me was the purpose of the company. Companies are transformed when they focus on their purpose. I did not want it to be used as a vehicle to create private profit and endless and exponential dividends that misrepresent the vision. I had a very deep understanding of the company as the medium to transfer an idea and purpose into reality. For me, it was crucial that the profits were reinvested and used for growth. When you get lost in all these complex structures and legal details, you lose track of your purpose and the actual value of your company that you need to develop.

Today, I can guarantee to our customers that they are investing in our purpose. We dedicate significant time and energy to spark playful movement for kids. Unlike many companies, where profits primarily benefit the owners, we reinvest the majority of our resources into realising our purpose.

If I had known about this structure at the very beginning, it would have been so much easier. I would not have needed to pay that huge amount of money to become free and to become a steward company.

Stephan Schenk, founder and managing director

6
STRENGTHENING THE BRAND

Every year, Reed holds long-service celebration lunches for colleagues who have spent 10, 20, 25, 30 or more years with us. People who stay for 10 years are given a bonus of £1,000 and a six-week paid sabbatical. The cash bonus doubles for those who have reached two decades and then goes up another £1,000 per decade. The sabbaticals are repeated too. As the boss, I am always there to host the lunches and mark these important milestones because this is an integral part of our company culture. In the last round, I hosted no fewer than seven of these events, welcoming over 100 guests to Tom Kerridge's excellent restaurant in London's Corinthia Hotel. It would have been completely unmanageable to get so many people into one private dining room at the same time and give them the individual attention they deserve. At each lunch I ask my guests to introduce themselves to the others and to say how long they have been with the company and why they have stuck around so long. The answers are illuminating and always include references to the people, the variety of the work, the opportunities to learn and grow and the company's purpose of improving lives through work, along with the fact that Reed is partly owned by a charitable foundation. People care deeply about this. They know that it makes their company different and they are proud of it.

The number of long-service attendees is remarkable for several reasons, but is perhaps most notable because recruitment is a notoriously tough space to work in. There is a lot of selling involved and there is no such thing as a quiet day. If you're the type to enjoy kicking back and relaxing, you will not make it in this sector. People tend to move around a lot, so the fact that Reed has such a loyal group of colleagues speaks volumes. Our PhilCo status is fundamental to this.

Even with such stark evidence, there will always be those who need convincing. People who still insist that the purpose of business is simply profit, and who, like Milton Friedman in 1970, refuse to look any further. Profit is, of course, a priority for any business, but here's the thing – a company's prospects can be greatly *improved* by taking a subtly different stance. Corporate philanthropy is not just about doing good works. It's a vital business metric.

There is ample evidence that businesses that integrate philanthropy into their corporate DNA deliver better results. More employee engagement; higher productivity; increased revenue, profit and shareholder returns; less absenteeism; better retention; and greater confidence in leadership. When people are engaged in a common purpose, it's to the advantage of *everyone*. Employees respond to the security of working in a stable environment and the certainty of long-term decision-making. There is even evidence that people who work in these companies are less likely to be convicted of a crime and less likely to get divorced. And it builds trust and loyalty among the wider customer base too.

There are multiple benefits to the PhilCo model, so let's look at a few in more detail.

LET'S GET ENGAGED

Employee engagement is falling. A 2023 survey by McKinsey shows it down 3 per cent on 2022, when it was already at a low level (32 per cent). Many people just quit, voting with their feet while leaving companies with the bill for recruiting and training their replacements. Perhaps more worrying though are the estimated 10 per cent of workers who remain and who are highly dissatisfied and actively disengaged, the so-called quiet quitters. These employees destroy value, not just by doing the bare minimum, but also by sucking the motivation out of those around them.

When the topic of employee motivation is raised, the most common response is that it is all to do with pay. Give people enough money and they'll be happy. This is not true – and will be even less so in the future, as research into Gen Z shows.

While money does help, there are many other factors that strengthen motivation. Workers are more engaged and productive when they know their efforts will result in increased charitable donations. Research also shows PhilCo ownership is associated with more employee stability, higher pay and better, more responsible treatment of employees, all of which combine to increase engagement.

The Swedish furniture brand IKEA is a case in point. The IKEA Foundation is the charitable arm of the INGKA Foundation, which owns the IKEA Group of companies. The goal of the foundation, which is funded by an annual donation from Stichting INGKA Foundation, is to create better opportunities for young people in some of the world's poorest communities by funding long-term programmes that can create lasting change. Along the way, it has improved access to education for more than a million children, provided clean energy to over 500,000 people, helped more than 20,000 farmers to increase their earnings and funded a huge amount of support for disaster relief operations.

The organisation is focused on encouraging everyone to buy into its philanthropic work, right from the start. IKEA's hiring process is geared to finding people who share its emphasis on values, competence and diversity. To join the estimated 219,000 co-workers around the world, people need

THE FOUNDATION THAT OWNS IKEA HAS HELPED TO EDUCATE A MILLION CHILDREN

to understand the culture and commit to the vision of helping others to live a better, more sustainable everyday life. The proof, of course, is in the numbers, and the rates of engagement are striking. IKEA is very highly rated in terms of culture and work–life balance, with 83 per cent of employees citing the firm as a great place to work.

Another interesting example is Maersk, which, like IKEA, was one of the ten PhilCos on my list in the previous chapter. When people think of Maersk, they probably conjure up a vision of giant container ships crossing the oceans. The words they might use to describe it are dependable and trustworthy, but these qualities are not necessarily that engaging for the workforce. In fact, it might make their jobs more challenging, as the necessary emphasis on safety, compliance and reliability may not be conducive to the most engaging of environments. Maersk is owned by the Danish PhilCo AP Moller, which donates a proportion of profits to around 500 charitable projects each year. Between 2017 and 2022, Moller donated DKK 5 billion (around £586 million) to these charities. In 2024 Maersk's employee engagement score was in the sixty-fifth percentile of Gallup's benchmarking survey and it has set itself a target of reaching 75 per cent by 2025.

I am sometimes asked in interviews to what extent we attribute our commercial success to our PhilCo structure. When I joined Reed back in 1992, it had a turnover of £82 million; in the 2023 financial year it had a turnover of £1.3 billion. The business has grown more than fifteenfold in three decades and outlasted many of its competitors. There are many reasons for this, but the most important one is that the people within the organisation care deeply about its future, its survival and its prosperity, especially because of what we achieve alongside our day-to-day work. They know that they play a crucial role in making the company money and, pleasingly,

HOW MANY SEARCHES DOES IT TAKE TO PLANT A TREE?

they also know that a large chunk of this money goes through the PhilCo to do more good work.

LET'S BE ATTRACTIVE

It's worth spelling out the impact on attracting talent. Our own research has shown that our PhilCo status plays a significant part in people deciding to join Reed. A good applicant might be weighing up two recruitment companies, but when they hear about our PhilCo status, they often find Reed the more attractive option. My sense is that this is a more powerful draw than a series of ESG initiatives because candidates can see direct change happening through our charitable foundation and especially through its relationship with Big Give. This matters a lot to younger recruits, which is especially significant. Gen Z, the generation born between the 1997 and 2012, will make up 30 per cent of the global workforce by 2030. To attract the very best applicants, employers need to engage with this cohort and create the kind of corporate environment they will be drawn to. That means one with purpose at its heart and in its DNA.

Like every generation, Gen Z have their own view of the world. After growing up with the news at their fingertips, they tend to have strong opinions about politics, the environment and what they see as fair or unfair.

When it comes to choosing where they work, salary is important but many other considerations may take precedence. On average, they would be willing to take a 19 per cent pay cut if it meant their non-salary needs were met. Three in every four of them (73 per cent) say they would leave a company if its business practices were unethical, 68 per cent would resign if they thought the business was not sustainable and 62 per cent would quit because of social differences, if the business was not believed to recognise diverse social groups based on factors such as gender, age, ethnicity and sexual orientation.

Much has been made of the 'war for talent', especially in certain sectors such as technology. There are simply not enough qualified recruits to go around and, of course, businesses always want the pick of the bunch. An alternative search engine, Ecosia, has had some real successes here.

Christian Kroll founded the company in Berlin in 2009 after a round-the-world trip showed him the damage done by deforestation. He structured his search engine as a for-profit enterprise, so his team could flex their entrepreneurial muscles and build the service, but the profits would go to tree-planting charities. Eighty per cent of the profits go straight to climate projects, with the other 20 per cent is held in reserve in case it's needed for business development. If not, the remainder goes to good causes too. Since 2009, Ecosia has planted more than 230 million trees in 35 countries. During this time it has built up 15 million users, many drawn by the fact that when they click on the ads that appear around search results, they are helping the planet to breathe. It takes 45 searches to raise the money needed to plant one tree, which is €0.22.

Ecosia, as you know, is up against one of the world's biggest companies. Google boasts 14 billion searches per day and invests heavily in tech innovations, spending millions of dollars to maintain that dominance. Naturally, much of the best tech talent wants to work at the cutting edge, developing products for the industry leader. Yet Ecosia is attracting top talent too. Tech innovators are quite willing to choose David over Goliath.

ECOSIA

STORIES FROM THE SHARP END

Ecosia

Ecosia is a search engine that uses its profits to fund tree-planting projects around the world. It runs on renewable energy and funds reforestation projects in over 35 countries.

Ecosia kept growing and growing and eventually we reached the point where we had substantial revenues. There were a few dozen employees and they started to ask about our plans for the future of the company. Was I planning to sell? When I told them no, I was not planning to sell, they said, OK, why don't we find a more legally binding solution to protect their future? As things stood, we were just a normal company that could have been sold at any minute. It was clear that, if we did, it would have been seen as a betrayal.

In 2018 we started looking for options and talking to lawyers. After going over many different models that the German legal ecosystem provided, and paying a lot of legal fees, we realised there was no real home for what we wanted to do. Then, eventually, one of our

119

employees said he'd seen something about the Purpose Foundation in a magazine. Purpose Foundation had a pre-pack process to implement what we wanted to do, which was to create a steward-owned company. It is not as good as a legal entity, but still something that is legally binding and irreversible.

Becoming a steward company turned a promise into a reality. I think it added to the company's credibility. I am personally always very disappointed by young start-ups that make big promises and then, a few years later, the company gets sold and the founders exit, forgetting all those big promises. I really wanted to make sure that this wouldn't happen with Ecosia. Even if I left the company at some point, or something happened to me, then it would be impossible that this could ever happen. The entire company went to the foundation and all the profits towards solving the climate crisis.

Most people join us because we have a credible mission, because we're doing something really impactful. They want to be a part of something. I would say that gives us a competitive advantage.

Would an employee share option scheme have been more effective? I'm a little bit sceptical about those types of schemes. I'm not sure that they set the right incentive. Most people who work somewhere like this are already motivated and don't need extra motivation. Sometimes people are a little bit confused about that, especially people coming from tech backgrounds. Maybe it kept a few people from signing. But then I wonder if maybe it is better that way. It is the culture of the company. Everyone at Ecosia is obviously very committed to the climate-change goal.

> Ecosia has helped start World Fund, a venture-capital fund that invests in climate start-ups, so I'm not against that model. It is now Europe's biggest venture-capital firm in the area of climate tech. We also proposed that they become a purpose-type of entity and they decided not to do so and that is fine. It is still a sister company, just with a different DNA. They too want to solve the climate crisis, just through very different means. If they have a successful investment, they earn some money, and part of that goes to climate projects as well. I'm not against this. Both types of company attract different types of people. I can only tell you in 10 or 20 years which was the better way.
>
> *Christian Kroll, founder*

LET'S BUILD A LEGACY

As the second-generation custodian of a family firm, a firm with our name above the door, I am quite interested in the subject of legacy and what a business and its founders will be remembered for. And more so lately, after a chance remark had me thinking. I was talking to Lauren Cohen, the LE Simmons Professor at Harvard Business School. It's not the first time I've quoted him because he asks great questions.

'When you hear the name Rockefeller or Carnegie,' he wondered, 'what do you think about?'

'Well,' I said, 'they were exceptional philanthropists.'

John D. Rockefeller gave away $540 million in his lifetime (1839–1937), which, at a conservative estimate, is $12 billion in today's money. Andrew Carnegie (1835–1919) gave away $350 million, worth about $6 billion today. Carnegie even went so far as to state that the rich had a *moral obligation* to give away their fortunes. But, if you and I were transported back in time, we might have given a very different answer to Lauren's question.

Rockefeller and Carnegie were known as robber barons. Among the exploitative practices laid at the door of such businessmen (for it was always men) were unfettered consumption and destruction of natural resources, unfair competition, undue influence on government and policymakers and dubious schemes to sell stock at inflated prices. Once they had made all this money, and perhaps seeing the error of their ways, they then set about giving much of it away, enabling their reputations to make a handbrake turn.

This is not to advocate that business owners behave badly in their formative years and then jump in to do a few good deeds later. It just shows the power of philanthropy when it comes to building a reputation. It really does create a legacy that can stretch far into the future. While Microsoft has changed the world in many ways and is now the world's most valuable company, I am quietly confident that what Bill Gates will be most remembered for is the Bill & Melinda Gates Foundation, which has given away $71 billion between 2000 and 2024 to funding healthcare and education and alleviating poverty: that is the true legacy of Bill Gates.

The PhilCo model can mould the legacy of a business from day one. Many of the organisations highlighted here chose their PhilCo status from the early days. Hans Wilsdorf, the founder of the luxury watch brand Rolex, established the Wilsdorf Foundation in 1945: it is the sole owner of Rolex SA, with 100 per cent of the shares. Rolex reinvests most of its profits into the business, to make more watches, hire more employees and do more marketing, such as sponsoring the tennis at Wimbledon. But the rest goes to charitable causes in education, science and the arts, as well as general investment into the watchmaking industry. Rolex has a reputation as more than a luxury watch brand: it has also proved its commitment to making a positive impact on the world.

A positive reputation is, of course, crucial to any brand. This is why businesses spend a fortune on marketing and branding exercises. Sustainability and social impact are more important values to customers today and can be the reason why they choose one brand over another. We have had feedback from Reed clients saying that our PhilCo status had a bearing on their decision to partner with us. They have seen reports of our charitable initiatives, which has reflected well on us. There is also a recognition that the income from some of their business will go through this structure to reach good causes.

LET'S LISTEN TO THE FOUNDING FATHERS

The structure of a PhilCo means its original values are more likely to become an integral part of its DNA. The Danish beer giant Carlsberg, with its memorable strapline 'probably the best lager in the world', is a great example of this. The company is one of the world's oldest PhilCos. When Jacob Christian Jacobsen founded his brewery in 1847, he had firm views about society and the importance of being an active citizen in a world in constant flux. Deciding he wanted to make his wealth do some good, he established the Carlsberg Foundation in 1876, bequeathing all of his property to it, including his brewery.

In accordance with his wishes, the Carlsberg Foundation gives the dividends from shares in Carlsberg AS back to support research into natural science, social science and the humanities, and grants funds to socially beneficial purposes, especially those that support young people. In the intervening years, there have been many company leaders who have come and gone, both from the family and outside. However, thanks to the original structure of the PhilCo, and its carefully documented vision, the philosophy has remained the same. The thoughts and ideas of J. C. Jacobsen are still upheld after 150 years, helping to give the company a clear direction. In the face of this solid foundation, it is difficult for a rogue executive to upend things or diminish the company's standing.

LET'S STICK TO OUR BRICK-MAKING

If you ask someone in business to list some companies with innovation and creativity at their core, the chances are they will soon come up with the name Lego. Somehow, despite the rise and rise of games on screens, this privately owned Danish company continues to grow. It is the world's largest toy company by revenue, bringing in more than $9 billion (£6.8 billion) a year. And, yes, it is a PhilCo. The Lego Foundation owns 25 per cent of the business.

Lego was founded in 1932 by Ole Kirk Christiansen, a carpenter in his forties who felt that, even in a depression, people would still buy toys for their children. The bricks were wooden at first, then plastic from 1946. At the heart of Lego's success are the core values Christiansen laid down – imagination, creativity, fun, learning, caring and quality. These themes have carried on from generation to generation. They were the foundations that underpinned this much-loved brand.

Something I find particularly interesting is what happened when Lego lost its way in the late 1990s. By 2002/3 sales had plummeted by 30 per cent year on year, Lego was $800 million

Foundation-owned Companies' survival after 40 years

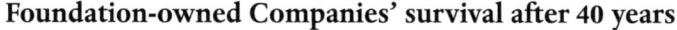
— Foundation owned   --- Other owners   — Other owners large firms

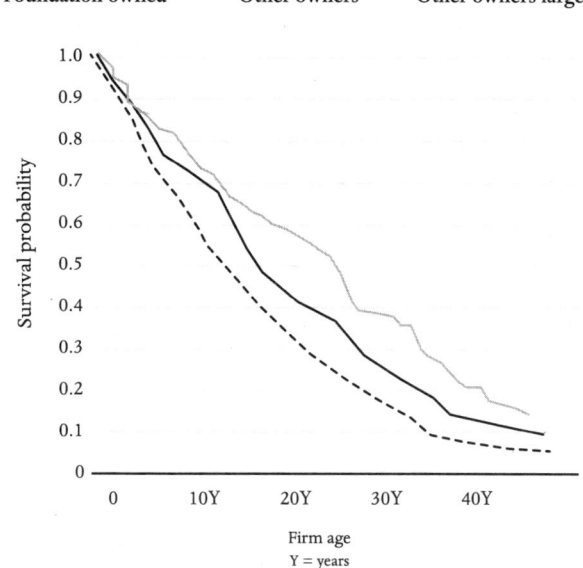

in debt and there was a period of panic when the consultants were called in.

These consultants advised diversification, so Lego duly introduced jewellery and a branded clothes line, a video-games division and theme parks. It was a disaster and the company haemorrhaged even more money.

Had it not been a PhilCo, it might well have been vulnerable to predators. Instead it was able to pull out all the stops, to innovate its way out of trouble rather than capitulating. The way the then CEO, Jørgen Vig Knudstorp, transformed Lego's fortunes has been called 'the greatest turnaround in corporate history'. There is even a book on the subject, *Brick by Brick: How Lego Rewrote the Rules of Innovation and Conquered the Global Toy Industry*. If you read it, you'll be in good company.

Businesses from Sony to Adidas and Google are said to refer to it for ideas on innovation.

Innovation has been repeatedly identified as crucial to sustaining long-term growth and profits. And what kills innovation? Short-term thinking, fear of failure, not giving time to let ideas develop, a lack of available resources. All factors that, as I've shown, can put the longevity of a business into jeopardy.

Research shows that PhilCos are more innovative. In Denmark, companies with this structure are responsible for more than 50 per cent of investment in research and development. This has a knock-on impact on performance. Again, this is the benefit of long-term thinking.

LET'S BUILD UP RESILIENCE

The evidence is that PhilCos are good businesses, both in terms of efficiency and resilience. This resilience can come into its own during an economic downturn, which is when you really need a business to step up. One study showed that, during the 2008–9 financial crisis, PhilCos were more resilient and less likely to resort to mass redundancies. This keeps businesses stable and better equipped to tackle the issues that arise as a result of straitened circumstances. Then, when the economy settles, they recover more quickly (see page 130).

There are many underlying reasons for this resilience. As I've said, people tend to stay at Reed for decades, because they believe in it. It works both ways. We are intensely loyal to our co-members, doing all that we can to preserve jobs in downturns and to support colleagues at times of difficulty. Also, we are frugal as a company. When we spend money, we try to spend it wisely and we avoid debt because one of our founding principles is to keep money going to good causes.

Paying interest isn't in this category. Helpfully, when a down-turn hits, this means we are not struggling under the burden of debt.

But there is more to resilience than just holding out in the bad times. It's also needed to protect the initial vision of the company. The founders of PhilCos have a greater assurance than their investor-owned counterparts that their vision for the firm's structure, direction and future will not be undone by activist investors or hostile corporate raiders. This can encourage future generations to put more effort in, too, because they know it will not be easily unravelled. They often feel proud to be presiding over a firm's heritage and to be personally identified with its ongoing impact.

Growing up I remember feeling pride in my family's charitable activities. One of my earliest memories is of visiting a farm in a remote corner of Cornwall with my father. He had bought Keveral Farm as a rehabilitation centre for recovering drug addicts, and a small community had settled there. One of the residents gave me a wooden jigsaw that he had made himself. I remember being both touched and impressed in equal measure.

Fast-forward 50 years and I know that my own children are also proud and impressed by their grandfather's philanthropic achievements. Most recently, when Big Give's 2024 Christmas Challenge raised £45 million in one week, surpassing Comic Relief and Children in Need as the UK's biggest charity fund-raising campaign, I would be lying if I didn't admit that it made me feel good.

Maintaining the vision was the reason why the founders of BuurtzorgT, the Dutch mental-healthcare services provider, decided to make their company a PhilCo. The firm had been set up in 2006 by Nico Moleman, a psychiatrist, and Jos de Blok, a nurse. In 2020 they switched to a PhilCo structure to

Foundation-owned Companies are more profitable compared to the Control Group

— FoCs ··· nFoCs

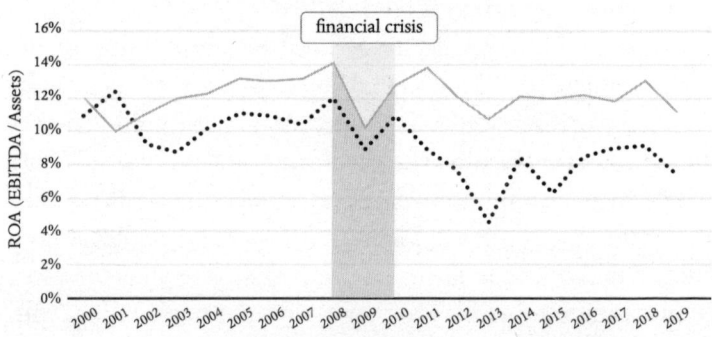

protect their concept for a transformative approach to psychiatric care.

The pair had started the business with the idea of finding new ways to help people battling mental illness. Their 'self-steering' strategy is based on creating independent local teams to give patients care in their own homes, rather than the traditional top-down approach, whereby a workforce is directed by leaders disconnected from the end user. Each team is responsible for everything in its own patch, from organising and providing care to monitoring their own financial performance.

The idea was so successful that the company achieved 40 per cent growth year on year and was providing care for 80,000 people. But with the founders nearing retirement and also seeking investment to grow the business, protecting the vision was very much on their minds. The solution was to work with Purpose Foundation and Purpose Evergreen Capital to transfer all the shares in the company to achieve PhilCo status. In the new structure, BuurtzorgT's employees are elected as stewards to set the direction and protect the vision. The stewards have 99 per cent of voting rights, with one Golden Share held by the Purpose Foundation, to give it a veto over any changes to the company's charter.

STORIES FROM THE SHARP END

BuurtzorgT

BuurtzorgT is a pioneering healthcare organisation established in the Netherlands in 2006. It is known for its innovative, nurse-led model of holistic community care.

Mental healthcare is becoming more and more organised. It is like there are factories of mental-healthcare provision, with managers closely controlling the inputs and outputs. That doesn't work in mental health.

Each case is unique and you can't make procedures and protocols to treat all cases. The important people here are the psychologists and the psychiatrists, who have the craftsmanship. This is why self-steering works so well.

Investors don't come in for the impact or the content. They come for the money. They would inevitably sell their shares in five or six years and the next investors might not agree with the self-steering concept. They would want to control the company in a different way, cutting costs and requiring more from employees so they could make more profit. I've seen that happen with a lot of mental-health companies. We didn't want that. We had a wish to preserve our way of working and treating colleagues, and the soul of our organisation. We thought, the company is managed by itself, so why shouldn't it be owned by itself?

This structure has worked so well. It is the stewards who have the voting shares and who decide where the organisation goes. This has been a way of giving the power back to mental-health organisations. I have never had such a relaxing time as a CEO! Normally, I would be very busy organising and implementing everything, but most of the work was done by the teams themselves.

Nico Moleman, founder and chief executive

LET'S GET SOME SATISFACTION

For the final point, perhaps a little selfishly, I want to highlight what being at the helm of a PhilCo has done for me on a personal level. It has continually invigorated my interest in the business and its place in the world. That is pretty inspiring. As any boss knows, being in charge can be lonely. This is not a cue for the world's smallest violin, because the advantages far outweigh the downside. Leading a PhilCo is a privilege, not least because it is so personally fulfilling. I love my job for all sorts of reasons, but underpinning them all is the knowledge that collectively we are doing something truly worthwhile. This is what I love the most.

When I go out into the wider world to speak at conferences or seminars, I often find myself being sought out and thanked by people whose organisations have received support from the Reed Foundation. They take the time to tell me what a difference the money has made. I haven't done anything to help these causes specifically, aside from running our company as well as I can, which is basically my job. Again, I would be lying if I said it didn't make me feel good. There can, and should, be so much more to running a business than just making a profit. It is great to make a tangible difference to people's lives.

Hearing about the causes the foundation supports also exposes me to all sorts of new and interesting challenges and opportunities. Often they're not commercial, but have great value from a social and environmental viewpoint. It's life-enriching to hear about activities going on outside my usual sphere.

A recent example is the £1 million grant made by the Reed Foundation to the charity UK Youth to investigate why anxiety and depression seem to be keeping a large number of young people away from work, and then to do something about it. UK Youth were the winners of a keenly contested competition run by the Foundation to mark my father Sir Alec Reed's ninetieth birthday. I found the whole process and, in particular, the dedication of the winners to addressing this serious social problem, completely absorbing and inspiring.

PART FOUR
HOW TO CREATE A PHILCO

7
CHOOSING THE RIGHT MODEL

Something that my father once said about giving to charity has long stuck in my mind. He mentioned that part of the motivation behind setting up the Reed Foundation and Big Give was because he hated the constant requests for money. It was not that he didn't want to give, he very much wanted to do something, but it was everything else that went with it. The lengthy fundraising events, with all sorts of different ways to get attendees to pop a tenner into an envelope, or bid a much bigger sum for an experience they didn't really need or want. Big Give was, he said, just cleaner. Plus, it made donations go a lot further.

Like most great ideas, the PhilCo model has taken a bit of experimentation to get it right. Fortunately, this process of trial and error happened more than a century ago. One of the pioneers was appliance manufacturer Bosch, which was founded in 1886 and now has more than 400,000 employees globally. For those interested in finding a better way to do business, theirs is an interesting backstory.

Founder Robert Bosch always prioritised finding ways to serve society as well as innovating with technology. In fact, this engineer and businessman earned the derisory nickname 'Red Robert' for introducing an eight-hour working day in 1906 and for paying his workers at a rate 60 per cent better than his rivals. As the company grew and became more successful, his thoughts turned to what to do next. What could he do to ensure that the company that bore his name remained socially responsible even after he died?

Selling the company, or listing it on the stock market, was a non-starter. Investors are driven by the singular goal of maximising profits and raising the share price. They would inevitably ignore the core values in the rush to realise a return from their investment. There is little to protect a company, its workers or the communities it represents. Shareholder primacy gives two core bundles of rights to shareholders. The first is economic and the second is governance rights, which grant control over the enterprise. No, as ever, Bosch needed to think a little differently.

His first solution to this challenge was a disaster. He sold shares in Bosch to his managers in the expectation it would empower them to step up and protect the company's mission. To his surprise and disappointment, the managers began to behave just like the very investors he was so wary about. They became fixated on short-term goals. Every initiative was tested against the potential for immediate financial gain, without a backward glance to consider how it might impact anyone else. These get-rich-quick ideas did no favours at all to the workers, or indeed, wider society. Bosch abandoned the experiment, bought back the shares and returned to the drawing board.

The next solution he toyed with, but ultimately decided against, was to give his shares to family members. While it might seem reasonable to expect that your flesh and blood would share your vision, there are never any guarantees. At best, his peers and even the next generation might share the enthusiasm for social responsibility. After all, they knew Robert Bosch and had no doubt heard his passion for the subject. Yet subsequent generations might have different motives, from him or from each other. In-fighting might break out. Eventually, this would destroy not only the ethos of the business, but also the unity of the family.

Bosch's third attempt was the winner. He devised what was to become one of the earliest modern PhilCo models. It was a structure that met three critical needs: security for his heirs, the protection of his core values and ensuring that future leaders would not be able to succumb to temptation and put short-term profits above these values.

It took a little time to realise these wishes, which were included in Bosch's will. That was mostly because he died in 1942, which was not the best time to be setting up a new company structure in Germany. But, 20 years on, the lawyers did eventually carry out his wishes and Bosch has since become one of the world's most solid examples of a PhilCo.

Since 1964, Bosch's foundation, which owns 94 per cent of the company, has spent around €2.3 billion (£1.9 billion). Today it supports more than 800 projects around the world in the fields of healthcare, the arts, research and teaching. What is really interesting, in the light of Robert Bosch's dislike of short-termism, is that the company has gained a reputation for long-term thinking. It responded to the dangers of climate change and put significant investment into green technology decades before other businesses began to react. The investments impacted short-term profitability, but it is well ahead of the game now.

COULD YOUR COMPANY BECOME A PHILCO?

How easy it is to set up a charitable foundation will very much depend on your current company structure. An established family business or private company is well placed to get on with it, since it can make autonomous decisions. With larger, publicly listed corporations, it could be more of a challenge. Conventional thinking seems to be that PhilCo ownership – where part of the company's shares remain with a charitable foundation – would be a tough sell indeed to the City or Wall Street. People have said to me that they would imagine that any CEO who mooted the move might find their stock value plummeting. This, in turn, they say, would make a business highly vulnerable to an aggressive takeover. I disagree. From personal experience, I do know it is possible.

When my father formed the Reed Foundation in 1986, Reed Executive was listed on the London Stock Exchange, having floated in January 1971. He simply bought the shares for the Foundation using the windfall from the sale of the Medicare retail pharmacy business. The Reed Executive business remained in public ownership, with all shareholders happily co-existing, until 2003, when I took the company back into private ownership. The family and the foundation retained their shares, while most but not all of the other shareholders sold theirs. The naysayers might say, ah, the stock markets were very different in the '70s and '80s, but that is not entirely true. Investors could be a pain in the proverbial even back then. There's a more recent example that shows what can be done. When the computer firm Raspberry Pi made its stock-market debut in 2024, its shares soared 40 per cent in early trading. This should be taken as a clear sign that traders were not the least bit fazed by the fact that Raspberry Pi is a PhilCo, with the Raspberry Pi Foundation, the charity founded when the company was set up in 2008, retaining a significant stake.

On the face of it, the most straightforward option of all is to decide that a *new* entrepreneurial venture will be built from the ground up as a PhilCo. Starting from scratch, a business could easily be structured as a PhilCo with an affiliated charitable foundation. But I would add a caveat here. For the most part, family businesses or private companies that decide to become PhilCos are financially stable. They are established companies, making profits, with their owners' thoughts often turning to the legacy they are creating. A start-up, by its very nature, is on a less stable footing. Very often investment is needed, possibly several rounds. It is challenging to raise capital, and some investors may need convincing that a proportion of the profit should go to a charitable foundation. These investors may never have heard of PhilCos, and, even if they have, they will almost certainly be more focused on realising a return on their capital. This doesn't mean the idea has to be put in the 'too difficult' box, but investors will need to be convinced that there will be gains down the line. The PhilCo path should be considered as a strategic part of the entrepreneurial venture's future journey with all the wider engagement advantages firmly kept in mind.

Related to this point is the sector in which you operate. While a strong argument can be made for businesses in any sector to explore PhilCo status, those in capital-intensive and highly competitive industries may need to think harder about timing. In markets like this, it is often first movers and those who push the most aggressively that have the advantage. A PhilCo might be at a disadvantage here for the same reasons that apply to a start-up. Sources of investment might not be as keen to get involved, which could slow down the launch process. The other side of this coin is companies in sectors that rely on customer engagement and trust, such as, say, wellbeing businesses or private healthcare facilities. For them, the PhilCo structure could be a powerful advantage. It's a shorthand that says: we care about you and what you think.

THE FOUR MODELS

Over time, the PhilCo model has become more prevalent, albeit better known in some countries than others. It's understood that a PhilCo gives a percentage of its shares to a separate non-profit organisation, which administers the charitable giving of that business. The non-profit is an entirely separate and independently run charitable foundation.

Why a separate foundation? Would it not, say, be easier to just agree that a certain percentage of profits will be given away each year? That is a compelling story to tell colleagues and clients, right? Apparently not. The boss of one PhilCo received rather a surprising reaction when he told a client that they would be giving away a percentage of their revenue. 'If you're able to do that,' the client said, 'then you are charging me too much.'

The consensus is that it is cleaner – and easier – to separate business and philanthropy. However, this does not have to mean entirely separate. There can be crossover between the directors of the business and the trustees of the charitable foundation. This can be a good thing too. It brings some continuity into the aims of the charitable foundation. In our case I am a director of the Reed business and also a trustee of the Reed Foundation. I am the only person to cross over the two; none of the other directors or trustees have this shared responsibility. My interest is publicly declared and I do not participate in decision making where there may be a perceived conflict of interest. This arrangement works well for us.

The first decision to be made when setting up a PhilCo concerns the size of the shareholding assigned to the foundation side of the business. When the Reed Foundation first acquired shares in the Reed Group, it bought 10 per cent, which has since risen to 18 per cent and may rise in the future. Some foundations own 100 per cent of the shares of the PhilCo they're connected with, while others have just 2.5 per cent, which I don't believe is enough. My view is that the best number to begin with is at least 10 per cent. This gives an instant motivational boost to the team, who can now say they are working half a day a week for charity. That is highly engaging, as we know first-hand. I would not argue against a higher percentage though.

There are a wide range of PhilCo models and governance structures. It might help to go through the most common ones.

1 Minority investor – the Reed model (10–20 per cent shareholding)

When my father set up the Reed Foundation, the impetus for it was a serious health scare, when he was diagnosed with colon cancer and given a 40 per cent chance of survival. One of the possible contributing factors was stress and anxiety from overworking, which caused my mother, Adrianne, to step in. She made it clear to my father that he must lighten his workload. They agreed that he would sell a subsidiary called Medicare, a 50-branch drugstore he had founded in 1974. Following a sealed bid auction run by the investment bank Hill Samuel, the Dee Corporation, which owned Gateway supermarkets (now Somerfield), had emerged as front runners. Dee was about to pay £20 million for the business and my father's thoughts turned to what might happen if he did not beat his cancer. Much of the £5 million he would personally receive on completing the sale looked set to be swallowed up in tax and death duties. He wanted to have something to show for the work he had put into building Medicare and to leave an enduring and meaningful legacy. His solution was to create the Reed Foundation, which he did by donating the £5 million he had made personally from the sale to a charity that he had previously set up, called Reed Charity. Reed Charity then became the Reed Foundation.

At the same time, a competing recruitment firm which had built up a stake in Reed, perhaps with a view to acquiring

THE MANTRA STUCK AND EVERYONE FOUND IT HUGELY MOTIVATIONAL

the company, let it be known that they would like to sell their shares. The Reed Foundation stepped in and used a portion of its newly acquired funds to buy them out. This is how 10 per cent of the Reed Group's shares came to be held by the Reed Foundation. Over time this increased to 18 per cent, giving rise to the mantra that our co-members, as Reed's employees are known, work one day a week for charity.

You could say we became a PhilCo by accident but, as we progressed, we began to see that we had stumbled across something truly impactful. Our team fully embraced the idea that their organisation was so active in the charitable sector. The mantra stuck and everyone found it hugely motivational. Just to be clear, we are not physically volunteering, painting nurseries or shaking tins outside supermarkets. We are each focused on our job in the knowledge that if we do it to the best of our abilities, the business will make more profit and 18 per cent of that will go to good causes.

How, then, does this minority-investor model work? The charitable foundation owns at least 10 per cent of shares in the PhilCo, but no more than 20 per cent. The foundation does not necessarily have an active voice in the running of a business. But it does benefit from the valuable contributions made by the workers within the PhilCo, and both organisations benefit from the synergies they achieve together.

The profits derived from the shares are a charitable foundation's principal source of income. Reed Foundation received dividends from Reed Global, the holding company of the Reed Group, of over £3.6 million in 2022 and £1.8 million the following year. Reed Global also provides free administrative support for the Reed Foundation, as well as volunteers from within the main business. Three family members, including me, are trustees of the foundation. There are also two independent trustees.

2 Investor plus – Raspberry Pi
(20–49 per cent shareholding)

The next option is an investor-plus model, whereby the charity owns a minority stake – but more than 20 per cent of the shares – in the PhilCo.

Raspberry Pi is a great example for a number of reasons. The PhilCo connected with it, RP Ltd, started out as a 100 per cent-owned commercial subsidiary of a charitable foundation. In 2024, when Raspberry Pi listed on the London Stock Exchange, the foundation's share stake was reduced to 46.7 per cent. This shows two things. First, the PhilCo model can be applied to listed companies, and secondly, the model can be flexible when needed.

The Raspberry Pi Foundation started life in 2008 with the idea of creating low-cost, programmable computers to inspire children to explore the joys of coding and creating with technology. The initial vision was that the company would make 10,000 to 20,000 devices and they would be distributed to young people, with the intention of inspiring some of them to study engineering and computer science. The founders set it up as a charity because they started with a wholly educational mission and didn't anticipate the commercial potential of the product. Yet, sales soared. It was not just children, everyone from hobbyists to industrial users wanted to get their hands on a Raspberry Pi computer. In the words of one founder, 'it got out of control'.

RP Ltd was set up as a subsidiary in 2012 and a portion of the profits from the business were distributed into the foundation. Between 2012 and 2022, around £40 million of profits were transferred to the foundation through what is know in the UK as Gift Aid. Over the same period, the foundation also raised a similar amount through grants, donations, sponsorship and selling educational services. While legally and practically separate organisations, they shared a common aim. The money has been used to advance computer-science education, particularly for young people who experience educational disadvantage.

While the commercial business was successful, it became apparent that it would need more investment to realise its potential. For the company to grow, it needed access to capital. It was agreed an Initial Public Offering (IPO) was the way to raise capital for the business and generate liquidity for the Foundation. It is very rare for charities to seek to list a commercial subsidiary, and it was important to demonstrate to external investors that the company was a commercial enterprise. Even with the Foundation's reduced stake, they took some convincing that the business was focussed on commercial aims. While they loved the philanthropy angle, they wanted to be sure they were buying shares in a company that wanted to grow in value. This was all underpinned by a Relationship Agreement which clearly sets out the involvement of the Foundation in the company post listing.

Since the IPO, the foundation has been involved in decision-making on the same basis as the other shareholders.

STORIES FROM THE SHARP END

The Raspberry Pi Foundation

The Raspberry Pi Foundation developed a series of small, affordable single-board computers in the UK. These computers are designed to promote the teaching of basic computer science in schools and developing countries.

The Raspberry Pi Foundation is a charity that created a technology company and eventually we listed that company in London in 2024. One important challenge was persuading institutional investors that this was a real business, not a charity. Charities don't bring things to public markets very often and most UK-based institutions did not know how to think about a charity being a significant shareholder. Institutions with experience in Europe were more relaxed about it. They had a frame of reference because the structure is more common there. One of our objectives was providing reassurance that Raspberry Pi was a fully commercial business and that the fact that it had been owned by a charity didn't adversely impact the commercial potential of the business.

The brand ownership was transferred from the Raspberry Pi Foundation to the company, in return for a commitment that the company would always make product available for education at specification and a price that is agreed with the foundation. That captured the essence of the charitable mission and we were very transparent about it. From the foundation's perspective, other than the commitment to low-cost computing, the priority is that the business maximises its commercial potential, because that generates value for the foundation, which ultimately enables us to advance our educational mission. The foundation owns 46.7 per cent post-IPO, so less than half, and we have no special rights as a shareholder. We have the same rights as everybody else.

One of the complex issues was remuneration. When the company was a subsidiary of the charity, it was subject to the Charity Commission rules and regulations around compensation that apply to all charities in the UK. We knew that in order to realise the commercial potential of the company it had to be able to compete for talent with other technology companies; our assessment was that required an element of equity-based compensation. We had to put in place an equity-based structure for employees of the commercial company, and that was probably the most complex thing I have ever had to do.

We wanted to make sure that the Charity Commission understood our plans and had an opportunity to raise any concerns. They got engaged quite late in the day and ran a very thorough process, which meant that it got quite close to the actual date of the IPO before they confirmed that they had no regulatory concerns.

Going right back to 2008, the founders of the charity (I was not one of them) had no idea that this would be something we might do. If they had, the articles of the charity could have been a little bit different, which would have made it easier. For example, most charities set up today have a standard clause in their articles of association that allow for trustees to be paid in certain circumstances. We didn't. That meant that we couldn't remunerate trustees who were serving as non-executive directors (NEDs) on the board of the trading subsidiary, despite it growing to a very significant scale. We were able to pay independent NEDs normal commercial rates, but not those who were also giving their time to serve as trustees of the foundation. Ultimately, we had to ask the Charity Commission for approval on a case-by-case basis, but that was time-consuming and could easily have been avoided if it had been considered when the foundation was established.

My advice to anyone starting a charity is that you should try to imagine the most successful outcome that you can and make sure that you've got the permissions you need to do that. Often the dialogue with the Commission is about trying to narrow your ambitions, when what you really want is the charity to be set up in a way that it can do extraordinary things.

Philip Colligan, (aka 'Phil Co') chief executive

3 Foundation-owned – Carl Zeiss
(100 per cent shareholding)

When you use your smartphone, you won't be thinking about PhilCos, but one that makes an essential component for such devices has been praised for having 'the ideal model of responsible entrepreneurship'. The business in question is the Carl Zeiss Foundation and those words of endorsement are from the former German chancellor, Dr Angela Merkel.

Zeiss, which makes microscopes and lenses, pioneered the PhilCo model whereby firms are wholly owned by a charitable or non-profit foundation. With roots going back to 1888, this is the longest-running PhilCo model. Also known as steward, trust or foundation ownership, it is most common in Northern Europe, where it can be found at Carlsberg, Anheuser-Busch and Lindt. In the UK, examples include Guardian Media Group, Andrews Property Group and Which? The structure can also be found in Asia, the US, Central and South America. Here, a company's assets are tied to the purpose of the company and managed by people who are not in a position to extract profits for their own personal gain.

In what seems to be a common theme, Zeiss's switch to PhilCo status was prompted by mortality. More than 130 years ago, following the death of Carl Zeiss himself, the co-owner of the business, Ernst Abbe, was left with a quandary. What should he do with his newfound 100 per cent holding in Zeiss? It gave him complete control over the company's finances, and he didn't believe this was fair. He asked himself: 'Have I created all this wealth?' His conclusion was no, it had been created by Zeiss's employees, generations of scientists and countless others. But while Abbe strongly believed that the

HE HAD COMPLETE CONTROL AND DIDN'T THINK THIS WAS FAIR

company belonged to its employees and society, there was, at the time, no precedent to recognise this in the company structure. This ever-resourceful physicist and entrepreneur invented one, donating all Zeiss's shares to a non-profit foundation.

Fast-forward to today and Zeiss is a thriving business with 70,000 employees. There are clear lines between the work of the core business and the work of the Carl Zeiss Foundation. They are controlled by two different boards. One has complete entrepreneurial control while the other oversees the charitable goals. This ensures that Zeiss, and any other company 100 per cent owned by its charitable foundation, can serve the public and the planet, without losing their independence or flexibility as entrepreneurs.

The foundation plays several roles here. One is to oversee the distribution of profits from Zeiss, which are used to support science, education and healthcare causes worldwide. Another is protecting workers' rights and guaranteeing fair wages. A third is to protect against the sale of the company, which is great for long-term stability. One of its more unusual policies, in a world where success appears to be marked by the size of a pay packet, is ensuring that no one at Zeiss earns more than 12 times the salary of the lowest-paid employee. This is, of course, very low when compared with pay ratios elsewhere. The European average is 110 times.

4 Double foundation – Patagonia (100 per cent shareholding)

Patagonia is a fascinating company, even if you're not as interested in mountaineering as I am. Its founder, Yvon Chouinard, turned his passion for rock climbing into one of the world's best-known sportswear brands. He lived out of his van at climbing sites for years as he built the business, which is based in California. In 2022, as its fiftieth birthday approached, Patagonia made a dramatic announcement: 'As of now, Earth is our only shareholder.' Every year the money Patagonia makes *after* reinvesting in the business is distributed to a non-profit to help fight the environmental crisis.

The vehicle chosen to do this is a double foundation, which, as the name suggests, means there are two separate foundations. This is to ensure that the independence between PhilCo and foundation is watertight. With the single-foundation model, there can be a perception that there is at least some risk of a company being overly encouraged to fulfil the needs of the charitable cause, instead of being 100 per cent focused on the business. However, opinions are divided on this point. Many experts feel the single foundation model is more than enough. Control over the aligned business cannot be bought or inherited. Dividend and voting rights are also separate, so no one can profit from short-term, profit-led decisions.

In this model, each foundation has a different role, separating voting and economic rights. The separation of power (voting rights) and money (economic rights) provides another layer of protection to make sure any decisions made by the foundation are never based on the personal interests of anyone within the business, and vice versa. There can be absolutely no chance of any blurring of incentives to prioritise profit over purpose.

This double foundation is the same vehicle chosen by Bosch. In Patagonia's case, the founder's family donated 2 per cent of all stock and decision-making authority to Patagonia Perpetual Ownership Trust, which oversees the company's mission and values. The other 98 per cent of the stock went to the non-profit Holdfast Collective, which aims to use 'every dollar received to fight the environmental crisis, protect nature and biodiversity, and support thriving communities'. Each foundation can block the other from selling shares, with or without voting rights, to outsiders. This protects the PhilCo – and its mission – for the long term.

CHOOSING THE RIGHT PHILCO MODEL

If a business is run well, it should, by definition, be good for society. As long as no one is taking out all the value that is created, the organisation should create prosperity for everybody. Karma capitalism takes that model a step further. PhilCo status makes a company a good thing in itself.

When choosing which of the models to follow, the starting point should be agreeing on the philosophy behind what you want to achieve as a business: your purpose. The other big question is, of course, how much of a stake company owners are prepared to give away. As I mentioned, 10 per cent is the minimum to become a bona fide PhilCo, but how far above that could you go? It's very much a matter of personal preference. I'm happy with 18 per cent of Reed's shares being with the foundation, although we would like to raise that to 20 per cent at some point in the future. It's a nice round number. Other businesses go all in, with the full 100 per cent of shares resting in the foundation. There is no right or wrong level, and no best option among the four approaches. It is what suits an individual company and its founders and directors best.

There are a couple of commonalities between the various models, which are worth noting.

Self-governance. No business wants to lose control over its operations, purpose or values. That would be self-defeating. Each of these structures is set up to ensure that voting rights are held by the people most closely involved in the PhilCo. These rights cannot arbitrarily be passed on and they are not vulnerable to speculators who swoop in to try to make a quick buck.

Purpose. The objective of a PhilCo is not simply to create wealth for shareholders. Depending on the number of shares assigned to its charitable foundation, a proportion of its profits will serve a greater purpose.

The process of weighing up the options is a good opportunity to agree on and lock in the long-term mission of the organisation, perhaps making social or environmental goals part of its constitution. Consideration could also be given to creating a class of share known as a 'guardian' or 'golden' share, which is assigned to the charity or foundation aligned with the PhilCo to give it a veto over changes to the main company's charter. While the golden share has no economic value, it can add another layer of protection to the mission.

8
ESTABLISHING A CHARITABLE
FOUNDATION

One of the biggest decisions every potential PhilCo will need to make is whether or not to set up its own charitable foundation. In England and Wales, this will involve engaging with the Charity Commission because you are legally required to register a charity if it's going to have an annual income of more than £5,000. This can be a fairly drawn-out process, with a number of criteria to be met, and can take a year or more. In the Commission's defence, there does need to be a balance struck between keeping the process moving and not making it too easy to register a charity, because then the system would be more vulnerable to abuse.

Before approaching the Charity Commission, it is crucial to have a clear idea of what your new charitable foundation will do. Some of the PhilCos I have spoken with have reported receiving hundreds of questions in response to their application. It will save a lot of time to figure things out in advance. This can then be reflected in a draft constitution.

DECIDING WHAT IT'S ALL ABOUT

While the senior team may be sold on the idea of becoming a PhilCo, there is the pressing issue that, if it involves a transfer of at least 10 per cent of the shares in the business, then somebody, or indeed a number of bodies, will need to gift those shares. This will usually be the founder, chair or CEO, as well as members of the senior team. In that case, it seems right and proper that this individual, or group, decides on the charitable goals to be pursued by the non-profit. It will be their hard-earned profits going into these ventures, after all, so they need to think carefully about how they'd like

PHILIP MORRIS GAVE $75 MILLION TO A CHARITY AND SPENT $100 MILLION PUBLICISING THE FACT

them spent. While the Reed Foundation doesn't play an active role in guiding the strategy of the Reed Group, the Reed family does have a say in the sectors it would like the foundation to support.

There are two schools of thought when it comes to how to spend the proceeds of corporate philanthropy. The first is that all donations should meet the strategic goals of the business. For example, a computer company might use its charitable giving to educate under-privileged youngsters in tech. It is, in effect, building its own workforce for tomorrow. The second approach is to separate the corporate and charitable activities and let the charity board make the decisions about where the donations will go, entirely independently of the company.

There have been notable successes with the first option, where the aim of the foundation is closely linked with the associated PhilCo. A great example is the Novo Nordisk Foundation, the wealthiest charitable foundation in the world. The main purpose of the $1 billion-plus it gives out each year is to boost biomedicine and biotechnology research, as well as general practice, family medicine and nursing. It is the owner of the Novo Group, which includes Novo Nordisk, the Danish corporation that manufactures and markets pharmaceutical products and services. Thanks to the company's success with weight-loss drugs such as Wegovy and Ozempic, the Novo Nordisk Foundation can offer help to people who really need it, at a price they can afford, where otherwise they might have been overlooked.

There have been pockets of criticism suggesting that the Novo Nordisk Foundation is concentrating research grants among its favoured causes. On balance, though, it is hard to argue with the tremendous good this charitable foundation does. Occasionally, some companies have come under fire for linking their charitable work with the strategic goals of the main business. Invariably, this is when firms have tried to use their donations in a rather clumsy attempt to improve their image, bringing us right back to the green/blue/pink hogwash discussed earlier. A clear case of this came when Philip Morris, the tobacco company, donated to a health programme in 1999. Just to add to that slightly uncomfortable feeling about the choice of partner, Philip Morris gave $75 million to the charity, but spent $100 million publicising the fact! So, naturally, some charities are wary of being used in this way.

STORIES FROM THE SHARP END

Bloody Good Period

Bloody Good Period is a UK-based charity that focuses on menstrual equity and the rights of all people who menstruate. It provides period products to those who cannot afford them and offers reproductive health education to those less likely to be able to access it.

We're absolutely behind the idea of corporates being more involved in charity. We need the support for our work to continue and it is a way of making a huge difference, especially to a small charity like us. That money makes a massive difference and so does the exposure to a new audience. It gets our brand into new places. However, the brand fit and values have to be right. Our biggest challenge is in actively building positive relationships with corporates that are aligned with us, and that is not everybody. We are a values-led organisation and have a very strict policy about who we will work with. There are companies that fall into a grey area that we need to present to our trustees for approval, and we do say no in a number of cases. We've said no to fast-fashion brands and we've said no to a vaping business. We say yes to others after lots of research, considering the relative risks and opportunities. There is an investment for charities to keep ahead of this and to really make corporate fundraising work.

Rachel Grocott, chief executive 2022–5

When it comes to greenwashing, or indeed any other colour of reputational laundry, supporting charitable causes for the sake of PR makes it inevitable that businesses will come unstuck, not least because nothing goes beneath the radar in the digital world. Even so, this is not to say that firms in difficult industries should shy away from PhilCo status. An argument could be made that adopting this business model would work in a company's favour if better presented. If you repurpose the drive to make more and more money for shareholders and realign the long-term purpose of the company to do something positive for society, surely that is a good thing, whatever the business does.

The role of a company is to provide society with a product or service it needs. Take, as an example, an oil giant. What is its purpose? To provide energy for its customers. But this is easily twisted, so it becomes: to make profit by drilling for oil. That is not a positive or compelling message, especially for those worried about global warming. But if this oil giant set up a foundation with the aim of using a proportion of its profits to create an infrastructure for alternative energy solutions, should it be condemned? Or should we look past the accusations of greenwashing to see that this would create purpose, prosperity and potentially something that is for the future good of society?

It can be a difficult decision and any potential PhilCo will need to think through all the angles before shareholders agree on the purpose of the foundation. When he was setting up the Reed Foundation, my father Alec chose the path of using its funds to benefit as many charities as possible. The beneficiaries, he decided, would not be connected with the main business in any way. As he had already given away a large amount of his own money, the Reed Foundation started by funding causes he already had a connection with. Since then, the process has become more formalised and the number of organisations has grown considerably. The Foundation has broad charitable objectives, focusing on funding a wide range of British charities. One of the things that my father strategically chose to do was support smaller charities that are often overlooked by the larger donors. This has ensured that many local organisations, often with dynamic hands-on leaders, have been able to increase their impact.

CHOOSING TRUSTEES

Charitable foundations are legal entities in their own right and are entirely separate from a PhilCo, with their own charitable purposes, governance and executive structures. The Charity Commission recommends at least three trustees, two of which must be independent. Trustees take ultimate responsibility for running the charity properly, ensuring it is solvent and delivering the outcomes for which it was set up. The Charity Commission says that trustees must always act in the best interests of the charitable foundation, *not* the PhilCo with which it is associated. Likewise, the foundation must be set up for exclusively charitable purposes that truly benefit the public. So that rules out an obvious PR exercise that is clearly there to further the goals of the main company. A blatant example of this might be if the PhilCo is seeking to move into a new territory and the core purpose of the proposed foundation is to provide grants to organisations there.

None of this is to say the charitable foundation must have a completely different brand identity. The Reed Foundation obviously shares the name of the Reed Group. This is perfectly acceptable and can even be advantageous since a PhilCo's company name may attract interest in the charitable side and its work. The foundation can also use the company logo in its publications. The only stipulation is that it is made clear that the two organisations are separate entities with different objectives.

When the Charity Commission decides whether to support the establishment of a charity, these are the main areas it will be scrutinising.

1. Trustees must be able to freely negotiate and agree funding terms with the PhilCo that will allow the foundation to pursue its charitable purposes. This includes being able to decline funding if there are conditions attached that are not in the charity's interests. The point is to protect its integrity.
2. Trustees must be free to take their own legal and financial advice, draw up their own policies and business plan, and conduct arm's-length negotiations with the company.
3. Trustees must be able to select beneficiaries and provide services within the guidelines at their own discretion. The foundation's charter will document the scope of its charitable goals – to provide support in education/science/the arts or whatever.
4. Trustees must be independent. They should never be pushed into a position where they feel forced to commit to the wishes of the PhilCo board, or to agree that an observer from the company attends confidential meetings.
5. If the foundation and the PhilCo are to participate in any joint endeavour, such as a publicity campaign, the foundation must show that any benefit gained by the PhilCo is a by-product of carrying out the charitable activity, not the main focus.

The Charity Commission is fine with a PhilCo finding and appointing trustees, either when the foundation is being set up or when a trustee resigns or retires. This can be included in the terms of the foundation's governing document. It is also OK for PhilCo executives to be trustees, providing they are impartial and follow rules regarding any conflict of interest. While I am a long-standing trustee of the Reed Foundation, I am not very involved in the day-to-day running of it. I am involved in the business of the Reed Group. I *work* to create income for the Reed Foundation. My job is to make as much return as possible for it. My father and my sister, Alexandra Chapman, who is the chair of trustees, typically decide where the money is going to go, or how it could best be used. I joke with my sister that I am the income department, and she is the spending department. She's always pushing me for more.

As a starting point, we would look for trustees with relevant experience. If the charitable purpose of the foundation is to support the arts, it makes sense to appoint people who know about that world, and about philanthropy. It can also help to bring in people from complementary disciplines to secure a range of viewpoints and avoid groupthink. The Reed Foundation has five trustees from a range of backgrounds who all contribute to the ideas and development of the charity. Big Give has eight trustees.

Personally, I like to have a number of individuals with experience in the business world, rather than purely the charity sector. I believe that business engagement is almost always a benefit for the charities. Typically, people with this background are used to getting things done, which means that they bring energy and ideas in support of their charity colleagues and to the benefit of everyone. Trustees also need to be committed to the foundation's goals and capable enough to evaluate its performance and to ensure that it is being properly run. This final point is, of course, crucial. Given the foundation often bears the family or business name, any reputational damage on the charity side will have an impact on the whole organisation. And of course vice versa.

Trustees must be made fully aware upfront of what they are letting themselves in for. The position is unpaid, except for reasonable expenses, which I should mention our trustees never claim. Additionally, if they act imprudently or in breach of the law or the governing directives of the foundation, they can be held personally liable for making good any losses incurred by the charity.

PREPARING LEGAL DOCUMENTS (AND BEING PATIENT)

The final stage of the submission is to draft the application to the Charity Commission. Drawing up these documents includes putting legal agreements between the PhilCo and the foundation in place, recording the foundation's licences, trademarks and intellectual property, and noting any shared resources.

After submitting the documents, it typically takes six months to a year for the Charity Commission to make a decision. During this time, there may well be multiple follow-up questions. Many will focus on the relationship between the PhilCo and the foundation, and any potential benefits received by the former. The long back-and-forth is the reason why I would one day like to create a plug-and-play model, which will help PhilCos get to the same place in a fraction of the time. We're working on it!

DONATING SHARES

There may be an alternative, less bureaucratic path. PhilCos can donate their shares to an existing foundation and let it get on with the distribution of dividends to good causes. Reed is currently exploring the potential for developing a broader PhilCo Foundation. This would be an off-the-shelf solution for companies that are interested in the PhilCo model but lack the time or resources to set one up. Interested companies would give at least 10 per cent of their shares to the foundation to qualify as a PhilCo. The income raised from dividends and Gift Aid donations would then comprise the foundation's charitable assets and be applied to its philanthropic objectives.

Once knowledge about PhilCos becomes more widespread, it will make a lot of sense to have one, maybe several, central non-profit organisations, where all sorts of PhilCos can assign their percentage of shares, regardless of their main business sector. This super-foundation would then manage the funds on their behalf. The idea has advantages over and above cutting out the administration involved for an individual PhilCo. It should also make for a much larger pot of money, resulting in far greater impact for good causes. Meanwhile, the administrative and organisational burden can be shared by a number of PhilCos.

There are a few considerations to weigh up here. The first is where organisations might prefer their money to go. To have a say in the matter, they would need to assign their shares to a donor-advised fund (DAF). This is a large charitable organisation that acts like an umbrella for a host of smaller organisations or individual philanthropists. You give them the funds and tell them what causes you want to help. If, say, you are keen to help rescue donkeys, the DAF will ensure your donations go towards helping donkey charities.

The alternative would be to donate shares to an existing foundation that is already dedicated to the cause you are interested in helping. If, say, you are passionate about digital education for young people, you could allocate a proportion of shares in your organisation to the Raspberry Pi Foundation. The advantage here is that the shares will be within an established foundation that is completely immersed in the core activity. It should be able to make the best use of any funds.

While it is a relatively simple process for a business to allocate shares to a foundation, there are tax implications. If the shares are existing ones, they will incur stamp duty, which is usually 10 per cent because this is a capital asset. The alternative is to create new shares, which do not incur the tax. If you go down this route, though, you will need to think carefully about the process. Generally, the board of directors can issue new shares without needing unanimous shareholder approval, but it does depend on the company's articles of incorporation and bylaws. However, issuing new shares will dilute existing shareholders' ownership, so many companies have provisions that require at least a majority vote from shareholders or offer them the right to purchase new shares first (pre-emptive rights). Also, any new share would automatically give the owner the chance to receive dividends or vote at the AGM. It is, however, possible to state from the outset that certain categories of these shares do not receive dividends and/or are non-voting shares. Nor is the recipient necessarily allowed to sell them.

Once again, it's a case of weighing up the options and working out what best suits your business and the wishes of existing shareholders.

9
HOW TO SPEND IT

Working out which causes a charitable foundation will support is a deeply personal decision and that is part of the beauty of setting up a PhilCo. It encourages dynamic people to engage in a whole different aspect of life within their communities and to support the causes they are passionate about. PhilCos can either choose causes closely connected with the main business, or they can separate the corporate and charitable activities, leaving it up to the charitable foundation to make the decisions about where the donations will go. This second route is the one we've taken at Reed. While doing the research for this book, I was interested to discover that the majority of PhilCos do it the other way, staying close to home turf. Both options are powerful, particularly when the money is made to work hard.

The first option is the more straightforward model. I mentioned Patagonia's recent switch to become a PhilCo, so let's check in with their experience of organising how funds are distributed from the newly formed Holdfast Collective. The company founder, Yvon Chouinard, was already a prolific philanthropist: he had instigated a scheme whereby 1 per cent of Patagonia's profits were given to environmental causes as far back as the 1980s. It was called '1% for the Planet' and subsequently more than 4,000 other companies have joined the scheme, resulting in over $728 million being donated to help the preservation and restoration of the natural world. The question for Patagonia was how to get the Holdfast Collective not only to replicate this work, but to build something much bigger.

Previously, Yvon and his wife Malinda donated their dividends to 500 different groups concerned with land preservation and environmental protection. The plan for the philanthropic donations tapped into this and created a funnel of around a dozen organisations at the top level in these fields. The Holdfast Collective then deployed a rolling window of resources to the chosen causes.

The underlying philosophy of the Holdfast Collective is that a $1,000 grant to a grassroots organisation is just as important as a $10 million grant to some other type of project. It does not sit back and wait for the A++ projects, where there may be the most bang for their buck in terms of biodiversity protection. Instead, its approach is: what's available now and what's really good? There will be another dividend the following year and that can be used to fund whichever pressing projects come up then. It's all about delivering the resources to what is most in need and has real value right now.

HOW THE REED MODEL WAS BORN

In the early days of the Reed Foundation, my father had a distinctly entrepreneurial approach to giving. This was mostly because he'd never been able to switch off the constant stream of ideas that came into his head. He often found himself attending a meeting of donors or trustees and his mind would drift off to how the charity in question could better serve its stakeholders. While he was on the board of the charity Help the Aged, he went on an away day to come up with ideas. Looking around the room before lunch, he noted that the major donors and decisionmakers were mainly men, while the recipients of the funds, especially in the developing world, were mainly women.

'If we were wise,' he thought, 'we'd give the money to women to spend. They're typically more honest than men and they will have a better idea of what the real needs are.'

For some reason there wasn't much appetite among the men to follow through with this idea. So he launched Womankind Worldwide, a charity that aims to bring about lasting change for women, and, in particular, supports women in Africa and Asia in their efforts to change discriminatory laws and social practices.

My father went through a similar thought process when he founded Reed Restart. He was at another meeting, this time about prison reform, and thought, 'I could do this better.' He approached HMP Holloway, which was then the main women's prison in London, and asked if he could put an office in there to employ prisoners. The authorities said yes, and Reed Restart began by engaging 50 women to stuff envelopes with fliers. The women were paid to do the job, which became the best-paid position in the prison. It went well and was emulated in a handful of other, smaller prisons.

Sadly, it only lasted a few years. It was not the near-escape of one of the prisoners that sounded the death knell. (She had hidden in one of the large mailbags carrying the fliers and ended up in the post van. It was soon noticed that she was missing and she was duly returned to her cell.) It was because of staff shortages that the prisons ultimately called time.

Another initiative that my father started was Ethiopiaid, which generates funding for local charity partners in Ethiopia. In each case, the £5 million stake he put in to launch the Reed Foundation was central to the founding and establishment of the charity.

His entrepreneurial approach extended beyond the very earliest days of the Reed Foundation. The early donations centred around the handful of charities he had set up, but by the early 2000s the charities were, in my father's words, 'running themselves', thanks to some very capable leadership teams. With his typical entrepreneur's restlessness, he started to look at what he

ONCE THE OFFER WENT LIVE, THE £1 MILLION WAS SPENT IN JUST 45 MINUTES

could do next. How could he grow the pot of money going to good causes? And how could he help more charities? The obvious answer was to get more corporates involved.

His reasoning was pretty simple. In almost every case, the amount of money a charity seeks from individuals, known as the ask, is low. 'Can you give £30 to protect/save/help X?' The ask may even be lower still – £20 or just £10. It takes an awful lot of those donations to make a difference. To make a real and lasting impact, donations needed to be far, far larger – the sort of money that only a very wealthy person, or a corporation, would have. My father decided that he needed to find a way to encourage others to do what he had done and pledge large sums of money. A £1 million donation from a high-flying executive, or a charitable foundation, could change everything for a charity.

He suspected that a large part of the reason that no one stepped forward to give significant amounts was they had never really been asked to do so. There was also a potential barrier in the absence of a central place where they could put their money and be confident in the knowledge that it was being properly distributed to good causes, with nothing going to waste. These were people used to investing millions, even hundreds of millions, in share portfolios, so if they were being asked to put large sums into a charity, they needed a clear and viable path.

After mulling over this thought for months but not really getting anywhere, my father arranged a meeting with some good friends and fellow philanthropists. They were all from business backgrounds and the idea was to see if some like-minded people could crack the problem together. They would have a mid-morning meeting, followed by a jolly good lunch once they had all cracked the conundrum of how to get wealthy people to put their hands in their pockets.

Well, that was the idea. On the day of the meeting, the minutes ticked by and there were no killer ideas coming forth. In fact, there weren't even any moderately interesting ones. Eventually they had to pack up because the lunch reservation beckoned. It wasn't until everyone was taking their seats for lunch that Mike Robson, managing director of Andrews Estate Agents, turned to my father and said, 'What you need is a virtual charity.'

My father didn't pick up on this right away, being slightly distracted by the fact that he was hurriedly seating his guests because they had arrived late for their table. But soon he asked Mike the obvious question.

'What is a virtual charity?'

Mike shrugged. 'I have no idea.'

They came no closer to cracking this over lunch, but Mike's comment did sow a seed. It prompted my father to have a website built, which he called Big Donors. It was an ambitious undertaking, with a couple of hundred charities invited to participate. They were each given a page on the website, to provide the information that big donors needed to know. The donors could access the pages and then donate, remaining anonymous if they wished.

He remembers it as a miserable experience. 'As far as I know, only one large donor even visited,' he says. 'They gave a quarter of a million, which was good, but not close to what I was hoping for. It was very frustrating.'

Not to be put off, my father decided to add an incentive. He declared that he would match the donation of anyone who gave money through Big Donors. A million pounds of Reed Foundation money was put on the virtual table. Once the offer went live, the £1 million was spent in just 45 minutes, matched by £1 million of big-donor pledges.

The idea of match funding was born. When donors see

that their cash can be doubled, it is hugely compelling. In 2008, the website was renamed Big Give.

HOW BIG GIVE WORKS

Match funding is the central component of Big Give and, thanks to the way it is structured today, it can turn a £1 donation into £4. In other words, whatever sum a philanthropist chooses to give can be *quadrupled*. It can even be grown by more than that. Basically, Big Give supercharges any philanthropist's and any charity's fundraising efforts.

To explain, let's break down the model. It begins with our Champions, as we call them. These are the wealthy individuals that my father was so keen to engage. Except that it's not always an individual. While Big Give does work with a number of individuals, it will often be a corporation, or a foundation or family office (which looks after the interests and investments of one or more business families) that wishes to support charities with a large contribution. Each of these Champions will pledge to donate a certain amount. They are putting the kindling into the grate, which can light the fire. The next step is to open it up to charities.

Charities that register with Big Give have different models to choose from. If they go for the 1:1, or Pledge Model, anything they raise through their fundraising drives will be matched pound for pound, using donations from our Champions. We describe it as 'double the difference'. We double the impact of people's generosity.

So if a charity runs a campaign to raise £100,000 from public donations, the Reed Foundation will put £25,000 into the pot and will ask them to find a 'Pledger' to match that sum – perhaps a local business or a charity's patron - to make a pot of £50,000. When the charity starts its public appeal, every individual donation made is matched by money from this pot, which doubles public donations. The original £50,000 pledged by Champions and Pledgers can turn into £100,000. It is not only a boost for the charity, but a compelling message to give to the public. *Whatever you give will be multiplied by two.* That means something even to people who hated maths lessons: every donation is doubled.

There is a chance to raise the level of funding even further. Adding in Gift Aid means the amount donated by the public can increase by up to 25 per cent. Also, when charities overshoot their target, rather than turn donations away, we often encourage them to seek out additional match donors. From the point of view of the Champions, the money they put up can end up being multiplied by five or six – in the example above, the Champion's £25,000 could be matched by £25,000 from the Pledger and £50,000 from the public, plus £12,500 from Gift Aid and further donations matched by the new match donors. And everyone naturally is delighted.

GO FORTH AND MULTIPLY

As you might imagine, match funding is highly motivational for anyone considering giving money to an appeal. Our own survey found that 84 per cent of respondents were more likely to give if their donations were match-funded. The average matched gift made through Big Give is £333, while the average unmatched gift is £132. One in three donors said the matching led them to give a larger gift.

Every year, Big Give runs eight different campaigns. Some, such as the Green Match Fund or the Arts for Impact appeal, are aimed at particular sectors, as the names suggest. We also have a structure to help charities launch their own match-funding campaigns. The biggest event of the year is our flagship Christmas Challenge, an online match-funding campaign that runs for a week in early December. It always goes live at midday on 'Giving Tuesday', the first Tuesday after America's Thanksgiving, which follows the Black Friday and Cyber Monday shopping fest. In 2024 it raised £45 million for over 1,267 charities.

Our Christmas Challenge, which opens for applications in May, is based around the double-matching principle, so charities need to find their own Pledgers to match the Champions' donations, which makes everyone work harder. On top of this, Big Give also runs emergency appeals as and when needed, such as the Middle East Humanitarian Disaster Appeal, which was launched to support the Disasters Emergency Committee's response to the ongoing crisis in the Middle East; the Indonesian Tsunami Appeal, which raised over £378,000 to help communities affected by the tsunami; and the Rohingya Refugee Crisis Appeal, which supported relief efforts for people fleeing violence in Myanmar.

The smaller campaigns are still significant. The most recent Arts for Impact appeal raised £2.75 million. We make it easy for people to get involved too. They can go on the Big Give website to give money or can do so on their phones through Apple Pay within seconds.

Over the years we have tried to make the process as simple as possible. Charities that want to take part in any of the campaigns register with Big Give and create an account. We then take them through the process of applying for a specific campaign.

An important feature of the process is that charities are welcome to use the platform to raise unrestricted funds. Elsewhere, fundraising opportunities are often confined to particular projects. A charity might be raising money, say, to build a new facility or provide a specific service. When we started Big Give, we received a lot of feedback that this could be quite limiting. Very often, the highest priority is to cover the day-to-day running costs of a third-sector organisation, so they can do their work. There is not always a compelling hook to hang the campaign on, even though the money is vital to the running of the charity. This can put many organisations off from applying for grants and funds. The funds from Big Give are, therefore, unrestricted, as long as charities meet our entry requirements.

Over the past 17 years, Big Give has raised over £340 million, which has gone to more than 5,500 charities. The amount grows every year and the goal is to raise £1 billion by 2030.

STORIES FROM THE SHARP END

FareShare South West

FareShare South West is a charity based in the South West of England that focuses on fighting hunger and tackling food waste. It aims to save good food from going to waste by redistributing it to charities, schools and community groups that support people in need.

The charitable giving environment feels a lot more competitive in recent years. During the first half of the Covid pandemic, a lot of trusts and foundations made record levels of grants – both in terms of number of grants and gift levels, despite their own interest rates dropping. Individuals and companies on the whole donated more too. The charity I was with at the time, a science centre, saw one grant funder donate nearly £1 million – up from the £10,000 grant they received prior to the pandemic. Although I remember it was interesting that, as a charity in the culture sector, but not an arts or accredited museum charity, we really fell through the gaps in both government and trust funding for the first six months: we needed to campaign to be seen and supported.

That level of funding dropped off pretty quickly after 2020 – it was an emergency response that wasn't sustainable long term. I think a lot of funders thought Covid and the effects of Covid wouldn't last as long and we would quickly go back to normal. But, instead, we've had the cost-of-living crisis stretching on and creating a 'cost-of-giving' crisis for charities, with more need and less money to go around. The emergency government funding has dried up and you see many trusts and foundations, whilst probably not giving less overall, changing their grant-making focus, going on pause to rethink their giving strategy or stretching their resources to support more charities, with either smaller gifts or higher levels of rejections than before. Your ask has to be more persuasive than ever, and impact measurement and relationship building are crucial.

Charities are faced with greater demand. At FareShare South West, we have a huge waiting list of community groups desperate to receive our food as poverty levels deepen in the region. We've grown exponentially to meet that need, but there isn't necessarily the funding to do that easily. We've done the Big Give winter appeal for four years now. The first time, 2021, we said, 'What if we can make £25,000 with our first appeal?' That was audacious then: it was more than we'd received in individual giving in a year pre-Covid. Then, the next year, it was, 'What if we can double that and get £50,000?' Then I arrived and said, 'What if we can double that?' Unfortunately, as competition for the Champion funding was so high, we were capped at £80,000 of match funding. We hit that target in the fourth day of the Christmas appeal, so that was amazing. And last Christmas we hit the £100,000 mark at last.

So, it shows that despite the economic difficulty, people want to help. People really value the doubling of their donations. I think match funding is going to increase in popularity moving forward, especially as people need to get more value for money when they're pinched.

Josie Forsyth, deputy chief executive

LESSONS FROM BIG GIVE

While it's intensive, running a match-funded fundraising drive is far less gruelling for charities than organising a major charity event. Setting up any large-scale event to encourage public donations requires a lot of work in a short time. Someone in a fundraising group described the process as being like going to Glastonbury: it's a great experience when it all works out, but you need a year off to recover. The fact is, organising any event is hugely labour-intensive. It often takes a team of at least five to set up and manage a fundraising event of any size. A match-funding campaign can be run by just one or two people and requires significantly less outlay. It's an efficient use of capital and resources.

This is not to say that charities should dispense with major events altogether. There's a school of thought that running them at the same time as, or in conjunction with, a match-funding drive can be very effective.

Obviously other PhilCos do not have to follow the Big Give route but, as has been shown time and again, it is a great way of maximising impact. The multiplier mechanism is a hugely effective device to support further fundraising. Here are some things we've learned since launching it.

1 THEY ARE THE CHAMPIONS

The model stands or falls by the number and quality of Big Give Champions. Many of them sign up and stay, and indeed gradually increase their donations; others come and go. This means there is a constant effort required to find new Champions. Some big donors understand immediately, but others need to be convinced.

2 FIST-BANGERS WELCOME

Big Give has worked with thousands of charities that cover a huge range of causes, addressing all sorts of social, environmental and health issues. What I find most satisfying about this is the incredible diversity involved. It is a really rich ecosystem. You may never have heard of some of the charities that sign up. Big Give is a really good route for people who want to give to good causes, but don't know where to begin. I suggest people ask themselves a question: what is it that makes you want to bang your fist on the table in frustration? It could be childhood poverty, or the isolation of the elderly, or the mistreatment of animals. There will be organisations addressing pretty much every issue on the Big Give website, many of them lesser-known charities that are crying out for support. Donations do not have to be restricted to one or two charities either. It is just a good place to start.

3   YOU GET OUT WHAT YOU PUT IN, AND SOME

My next observation is more directed towards the charities that work with Big Give. It is not a model that works for every third-sector organisation. While it might seem like an incredible opportunity to raise a large sum – and it is – there is an element of self-selection around the charities that make the best of it. Without a doubt, it tends to be the more dynamic charities that embrace this model, because there is some work involved on their part. It is not like applying for a grant and receiving the money, job done. Even with the 1:1 pledge model, the charity has to put on an energetic public campaign to match the donations pledged by the Champions. If they are going for the multi model, it requires engaging with major donors as well as the public to raise the 4x funds.

It can be Darwinian, because those charities where people might be complacent or less dedicated don't do as well as the ones where the people are more driven and dynamic. Once, a local theatre charity let it be known that they were 'too busy' to take part in one of our appeals. I happened to know the chairman of the board of trustees, so I mentioned this to him. He knew nothing about it and, when he found out, he was pretty horrified. The charity team was encouraged to participate and, as a result, raised £50,000, which was 100 per cent match-funded. Well worth a prod for £100,000 raised.

STORIES FROM THE SHARP END

Reach Learning Disability

Reach Learning Disability is a UK charity that supports people with learning disabilities to live fulfilling, independent lives by providing day services, community support, and supported living across Nottinghamshire. Through initiatives like Flower Pod and their outstanding-rated Reach Care service, they offer meaningful activities, personal development, and one-to-one support, helping individuals thrive within their communities.

It is a little bit difficult to get your head around the matching. Every year, I remind myself of how it works before I then start trying to explain it to colleagues, funders and supporters. It has become very much an established part of our fundraising year now and some of our supporters expect us to be doing it. They look forward to being involved in it as well.

A lot hinges on choosing the right project, something that is going to be attractive to a Champion and the initial pledgers, but is also going to have public appeal. I have learned over the years not to make the ask too complex and not to choose a complicated title that you're then going to struggle to communicate, either for your appeal or your project. We just need something that can be explained to colleagues quite simply.

Julia Sandhu, fundraising director

4   AND DON'T FORGET YOUR OWN COLLEAGUES

My final point is that it's crucial to engage *all* stakeholders. I mentioned the Reed mantra that our co-members work one day a week for charity, thanks to the PhilCo model we've built. We know from regular company surveys that this is a hugely motivational force and it builds on the trust culture within Reed. Our co-members trust that when we are doing work for a charity, it is going to the right places. You can see it and feel it when the Big Give Christmas Challenge comes around. There is always a noticeable buzz around the business at this time of year. It feels as if everybody is on board with it. This doesn't just happen, though. Good communication is crucial because we need to bring everyone along with us. We do our best to share the stories around what is happening, so the co-members can see the good work that's being done and the incredible sums being raised. One way we do this is by having Big Give's website on the screen in our office reception so that people can see the running total rise through the course of the week as they come and go. We also have regular updates on social media showing celebrity endorsements and fundraising progress. Christmas Challenge week is a big deal. Great things happen and great sums of money are raised for good causes thanks to a huge communal effort. People are proud to be associated with it.

PART FIVE
LET'S DO IT

10
BECOME A PHILCO

What is the point of business? Even CEOs ask themselves that. Milton Friedman's answer to the question – to make money for the shareholders – now feels dated. We've all seen how much harm it can do. There is a growing appetite for a new, more inclusive form of capitalism. Yes, making profit is still an important goal – but so is improving the outcome for all stakeholders. It means strengthening the economy and society as a whole, as well as looking after employees and customers.

With any big cultural shift, there will be a few wrong turns as we work out the best way to enact the change we want. The ideas behind the burgeoning ESG movement were well-intentioned but always vulnerable to bureaucratic capture, misinterpretation or indeed abuse. It has spawned a multimillion-dollar industry, but the good causes it is supposed to be supporting are receiving only a fraction of that. When something does not work as it should, it's very easy to point the finger and say it's a waste of time.

ESG has not only been dismissed as a waste of time, but has also earned the emotive epithet 'woke capitalism'. Interestingly, though, not even its strongest detractors have called for an unquestioning return to the shareholder-first model. There is an acceptance that while companies must pursue profits, they cannot ignore purpose. Stakeholders, from customers to society as a whole, expect it, and these are the people from whom those profits are made. In our new version of capitalism – karma capitalism, where the DNA of the business has changed and a foundation becomes a shareholder – businesses that work in the interests of *all* their shareholders will help maximise returns for all stakeholders. Everyone wins.

What has changed? Back when Friedman declared that shareholders should come first, there was a wider assumption that it was up to the government, not business, to rise to the challenges of creating a fairer society. In the days before the Internet and social media, there was a lot less transparency. Companies played their cards close to their chest, citing confidentiality and competitive advantage, and no one batted an eyelid. That has all changed. Anyone with a smartphone or laptop can now scrutinise what the companies we buy from are up to – and we use that information to guide our choices.

Since the turn of the twenty-first century, trust in our various governments has gone precipitously south. We are now far more likely to trust business than our elected officials. According to the Edelman Trust Barometer 2024, business is now viewed as the only global institution that is both competent and ethical. While this is good for business, it does come with responsibility. The same report found, by a six-to-one margin, that people want business to take the lead on societal issues such as climate change, economic inequality and workforce reskilling.

If we ignore it, will it all go away? Will we snap back to a position where business can safely leave it to governments to deal with life's challenges? It doesn't seem very likely. So businesses need to step up. Since the ESG model is flawed, we need a better way to appeal to stakeholders, a better way to get the job done. Karma capitalism, delivered through the PhilCo, is the way ahead.

Big change is coming. At Reed, we are investing in a new recruitment service, Reed.ai. This service will go live in 2025, thirty years after our first exploratory website, Reed.co.uk, appeared on the scene in 1995. The development was partly inspired by a conversation I had with worldwide web creator Tim Berners-Lee. Tim and I had been discussing the possible changes that would come with the arrival of AI in the business mainstream, when he said something striking: 'AI will be able to do everything you can do.'

Tim's words made me reflect on the essence of what we do. The Reed Employment agency, founded in 1960, is all about connecting people. How can AI improve the experience of our customers? How can we use this exciting technology to improve our business? We decided to build a new AI-based service that would be specifically targeted at the hard-pressed business owner who so often needs to find people fast and at a fair price. Up until now, AI has largely acted as an assistant. Our new offer would use it to deliver the service of an agent, to do the same job that my father did all those years ago when he opened the first Reed office in Hounslow.

We have already invested millions of pounds in this project. We don't know yet if it will work or if the customers it is designed to serve will appreciate it and pay for it. In some ways Reed.ai is a shot in the dark, but I feel secure in making such an investment because our business is a PhilCo, and Phil-Cos take the long view. Our new endeavour may not work for a while, or at all, but if we did not do it, would we be happy watching others pass us by?

Our commitment to research and development is deeply rooted in an entrepreneurial culture that goes right back to our founder and our PhilCo status. We are prepared to give Reed.ai a go in the knowledge that in five or ten years' time people will be hiring people and using recruitment services in radically new ways. Our PhilCo status gives us a degree of assurance that we will be competing in these markets of the future, so we had better get on with it and prepare for them. Otherwise, our fate will be irrelevance.

A few months after that initial conversation, I saw Tim again and I told him how his remark had galvanised me into action. He qualified what he had previously said: 'AI will be able to do almost everything you can do.'

The PhilCo model is the solution for the twenty-first century. It creates a new kind of corporation and a brighter future for capitalism. It offers a new and kinder variant – karma capitalism – which is much better suited to the demands of today's world.

Business leaders know how to run things. We know how to turn a profit, reduce waste and keep things on track. Corporates can change pretty much anything. As major players in our global society, they have an incredible opportunity to make a positive impact through philanthropy. The more they become involved, the better it will be for everyone else.

This new kind of capitalism will take a bit of adjusting to for some businesses. To reiterate, though, it does not challenge the notion of shareholder primacy. You can still see value for shareholders as your main aim. It's just that one of those shareholders will be a foundation – and you'll be caring about other stakeholders too.

STORIES FROM THE SHARP END

Reed

Reed group is a recruitment and philanthropy company that is primarily focused on recruitment, learning and public services

Quite simply, when we became a PhilCo, we began to see better results. Our profitability improved. What would I put this down to? Well, a combination of factors is at play here. Most importantly, our clients were very encouraged by it. They liked the idea that the company was partly owned by a charity. It set us apart. This was particularly appealing to our clients in the public sector, especially local government. What's more, our company became more attractive as a place to work so we were able to recruit better people, and these people stayed with us for longer and became more committed to the organisation. Becoming a PhilCo gave us all a real sense of purpose. It almost happened by accident following my cancer scare but the results have become obvious to me. We have ended up with a much better business.

There are no disadvantages that I can think of. Obviously, it all began when I gave £5 million to the charity back in 1986 but you can give away 10 per cent of the business in this way and more than recover it through increased profit. Added to that is all the satisfaction that arises from the philanthropy side. This has enriched my life hugely and much more than having more money would have done. I didn't need any more money.

I wouldn't hesitate to recommend the PhilCo route to other entrepreneurs and business owners. It's been brilliant for us. It's best to give the money to your foundation and then have the foundation buy the shares in the business, but make sure you get good legal advice.

Sir Alec Reed, founder at large

Something that came across strongly when I was researching this book is how the PhilCo model is better known in some countries than others. In Denmark, it is almost the norm and PhilCos make up a significant share of the economy, while in Britain it is still the exception. It's assumed that part of the reason it is more prevalent in Denmark is that a century ago the tax situation in that country was more favourable for this kind of company structure. A number of large companies, so the theory goes, made the transition to get the tax benefits. Over time, the idea gained momentum. The model was front of mind when new companies were being formed, so many adopted it. Wouldn't it be great to see that sort of momentum resume today, particularly in regions that have been slow to adopt this approach?

Any company can become a PhilCo, whether it's just starting out or is well established. How quickly, or easily, will very much depend on its existing structure. A family business or private company is well placed to just get on with it. Ditto a new entrepreneurial venture. When you're starting from scratch, it's straightforward to structure the business around being a PhilCo. Where things can become a little more difficult is when it involves larger, publicly listed corporations. But difficult should never be viewed as too difficult, as Raspberry Pi proved by changing its own original structure for its IPO. Big corporates are crucial to this new model. When large-scale businesses become PhilCos, we will finally be able to properly address the issues facing our society today. The success of the endeavour will depend on the team and how they engage with the PhilCo approach. Plus, of course, it will be vital to bring other stakeholders on board, from customers to charity partners.

While the title of this chapter, 'Become a PhilCo', is a call for action, I am in no way asking for government help. I'm not calling for tax incentives to encourage organisations to consider this route. Any tax benefits will come with a mandate to follow different rules. A PhilCo would be in the same boat as a non-profit, which has to follow strict rules. Reed is not a non-profit. We are a normal business that decided a long time ago to give part of its profits away. We don't want to be beholden to rules that tell us how and when we can do this. And we don't want you to be.

Governments do, however, have an opportunity to help create a new generation of charitable battalions. They can do this by lending their soft support to this initiative. It is in their best interest because of the many and obvious benefits to be gained from more businesses adopting the PhilCo model. There is a clear need for more support for the charity sector and especially for social care. Central governments don't have the means to do much more and are clearly struggling with the commitments they already have. But if they help business, business will help them. It is to governments' advantage if companies are more stable, innovative and stick around for longer. This will boost the economy, benefit society and delight the taxman.

Again, it is useful to consider the Danish example, since there are so many PhilCos there. After the 2008–9 financial crisis, the Danish economy was much less vulnerable than most to the 18-month disruption that ensued, in part because PhilCos are protected from opportunistic takeovers. Companies in a temporarily vulnerable situation cannot be so easily seized and their ownership moved overseas. So the ongoing benefit of the innovation and development of PhilCos stays in their country of origin.

Schools and universities should also become more involved in this sacred mission. When our educational institutions talk about business, they should lay out the different approaches available and highlight PhilCos. They should talk about the purpose of business and the wider good that it can do. They should examine how it is possible to run businesses for the good of society, just as some of the pioneering and public-spirited early capitalists first intended. If the PhilCo model is presented as the fair, equitable and intelligent choice that it is, I am convinced more people will choose it.

Overall, we need to create a more positive view of business. Too many people have accepted the argument that corporations are inherently bad, and only in it to squeeze out profits at the expense of the many for the benefit of the few. We need to reclaim the narrative that business can be an engine of progress and can be good for society as a whole. And we can take hope from the fact that there are many people who see the potential for business to be a positive agent for change. We will do this through a new battalion of firms who are dedicated to this new form of ownership. We will do this one PhilCo at a time. And by changing the DNA of individual businesses, we will change the DNA of capitalism itself. Karma capitalism is that force for good. Karma capitalism is the way forward. Now is the time to become a PhilCo.

11
FREQUENTLY ASKED QUESTIONS (FAQS)

I WANT TO START A PHILCO. WHERE DO I BEGIN?

Start by working out your purpose and how much of your business you are prepared to place in a foundation. This is all a matter of personal preference and appetite. After that, it is a case of creating a clear framework for structured and strategic corporate giving. There is no legal definition of a PhilCo, nor of a corporate foundation, nor is there a one-size-fits-all model to set one up. Our definition of a PhilCo is where a charitable foundation owns at least 10 per cent of the company. As this book has outlined, there are several options, but everything flows from your purpose and the size of your commitment.

WHY NOT CHOOSE EMPLOYEE OWNERSHIP?

Much has been made of the opportunity to engage with employees and, in particular, Gen Z, who are especially focused on people and planet. It is a fair question to ask whether employee share options and ownership might be an alternative option. The Bosch experiment is a clear indicator of what might go wrong in this case. Shares were gifted to company managers and, almost immediately, they began to behave like the proverbial fat cats. Their main motivation seemed to be to run the business to make money for themselves, never mind the broader purpose of doing good for society. They wanted to realise a profit in the short term, which is seldom good for the long-term health of a business.

The switch to PhilCo status involves fundamentally rethinking how a company interacts with the outside world and how it behaves towards its own workforce. What makes a PhilCo stand out compared to other ownership structures is that it creates a new way to look at a company for *everyone* within it. The idea of making a social impact is so important for employee engagement because it is motivating: it really changes the company and how everyone acts. The challenge is to ensure that the people making the decisions really feel aligned with what they're doing, that they feel good about it and that they are completely committed to the mission of the company.

IS IT JUST ANOTHER WAY OF SKINNING THE ESG CAT?

While the intentions may seem similar to ESG initiatives, certainly in terms of putting company resources into social and environmental good causes (depending on the goal of individual PhilCos), the implementation is worlds apart. And that is what makes it such an impactful option. Remember those five big holes in the ESG framework: lack of regulation and standardisation, incomplete or selective reporting, insufficient integration into core business practices, lack of accountability and lack of immediacy? The involvement of the Charity Commission – a legal requirement for the PhilCo model in England and Wales – addresses all these issues. Once a foundation is registered as a charity, there are strict obligations to keep accurate financial reports and to document and account for where funds are being spent. You can't make any vague and misleading claims, because there's a paper trail. Similarly, the funds being sent to the charitable foundation are there to be spent on viable and meaningful projects that are happening now, not at some vague moment in the distant future.

In our case, the money raised each December by our major fundraising drive, Big Give's Christmas Challenge, is with our charitable partners immediately. The PhilCo framework leads to almost instant – and meaningful – change.

Becoming a PhilCo offers businesses a genuine way to grow and develop their charitable giving in a way that will be of benefit to society. So, yes, this is much better than reams of uplifting words in an ESG report.

WOULDN'T LOTS OF COMPANIES ALREADY CONSIDER THEMSELVES TO BE PHILCOS?

Well, many businesses already actively engage with charities. They may make provision for employee secondments or volunteering programmes. They may also donate resources, such as allowing buildings to be used pro bono for meetings or conferences, or giving away surplus stock or machinery. Then there is hard cash, which can be given in a variety of ways, from one-off contributions to payroll giving to employee fundraising schemes. All of these are laudable and, indeed, crucial for the charity sector. But they don't make the business a PhilCo. The only criterion for this is that at least 10 per cent of the shares must be held by a charitable foundation.

Becoming a PhilCo implies a longer-term commitment, and the intention should be to make a more profound difference to one or more good causes. Here is the thing, though. PhilCo status is in a company's interest because it is less of a distraction to the main business than these piece-meal engagements and donations. Every company receives countless requests for donations. A PhilCo can redirect these requests to the foundation and get on with what it does best – in whatever sector it is in. Meanwhile, everyone can work away knowing that a proportion of the profits they make will go to good causes.

HOW MUCH WILL IT COST ME?

At the moment, there can be some significant costs involved in setting up a PhilCo and related charitable foundation, particularly if you go for the do-it-yourself version. In some regions, the PhilCo structure is still quite rare, so it will take time and you will need legal help. The good news is that it won't be anything like what it cost Bosch – you may remember that it took lawyers 20 years to figure out how to set up that foundation. It is eye-watering to imagine the bill from the 40-strong team of legal eagles. According to Purpose, which supports PhilCos (or steward-ownership as they like to call it) around the world, the cost tends to be around €250,000 if businesses take on the task themselves. This can vary from country to country and is spent on legal, tax and incorporation requirements. Purpose is aiming to vastly reduce the costs of all this by open-sourcing some of the key elements, such as the legal templates, for which it charges an annual fee of €500. This is on a country-by-country basis, because the rules vary by jurisdiction. At the time of writing, their templates are only available in Germany, but they are working on them for other countries in Europe, the UK, US and Latin America. Big Give will also host guidelines and templates to help new PhilCos. Setting one up is not a trivial process because of the disparities in legal requirements, but this should not be a barrier to getting started.

IF YOU CAN'T SELL A PHILCO, WHAT HAPPENS WHEN THE FOUNDER GETS TIRED, LOSES INTEREST OR IS UNABLE TO WORK?

The first thing to understand is that voting rights are determined by the number of shares held in the company. If a PhilCo is 10 per cent owned by a foundation, the founding members are likely to be able to vote for a sale in the face of opposition from the foundation, assuming that is their preferred option. This becomes less likely the bigger the share owned by the foundation. The larger the shareholding, the more likely it is that a prospective sale will also require the support of the foundation's independent trustees.

When a PhilCo is wholly owned by a foundation, the issue of sale or succession is entirely in that foundation's hands. This can be welcomed by some entrepreneurs because it allows them to create something new and then move on at a later date without losing whatever they created. PhilCo status protects the company and allows the trustees to make decisions strategically, freely and independently of the original founders.

In practice, there are very different options for deciding on succession and each company needs to find the model that fits best. Organisations should determine a succession mechanism before transitioning into a PhilCo. This could include appointing a succession council which would come together in the case of the founder getting tired, losing interest or being unable to work, or indeed the death of a founder, and then settle on the most suitable person(s) to take over.

I WORK FOR A BUSINESS – HOW DO I PERSUADE MY BOSS TO DO THIS?

Ask your boss which companies they most admire and then point them to the successful companies listed in this book and see if there is any crossover. Life is fleeting, and business life is especially so. The promise of improved performance, added longevity and an enduring legacy should attract their attention.

AFTERWORD

Changing the DNA of business one PhilCo at a time is not a trivial enterprise – I am fully aware of that. It can take time for good new ideas, even great ones, to become mainstream. Often this is because those good ideas must compete with bad ideas that might sound better at first, but on closer scrutiny they are revealed to have little true merit. Creating a new generation of PhilCos will not be easy and will take years. We may not reach critical mass in my lifetime (I am now 61). I do, however, believe that once we achieve a certain amount of impetus, this idea will develop a life of its own.

When you started reading this book, you may never have heard of the word PhilCo, let alone known what one is. My hope is that, even if just by giving an idea a name, it will encourage you to talk about it. When people begin to have these conversations, it gives an idea momentum. It becomes a mission, then a movement, and karma capitalism will grow.

Change won't just come from the people running businesses either. If you are reading this and are inspired by the idea of PhilCos, do tell your boss, your colleagues or your teacher or mentor and give them a copy of this book. If enough people say, 'Hey, why aren't we doing this?' executives will sit up and listen. I know that I would.

The ownership of any company has for too long been about money and power. Who holds the power in the business and why? And who should get how much money and why? From an individual psychological perspective, these are probably the deepest questions you can ask of a company founder or boss. And we should all be asking these questions a lot more. If we don't like the answers, we should keep on asking the questions.

Becoming a PhilCo is not a panacea. A business still needs to be well run. In fact, the success of the model relies on this. It is crucial that executives focus on good management and good governance – and the many things they should be doing anyway to ensure a business is successful. This structure will strengthen any business too. As an entrepreneur and leader of a family-owned company, I frequently speak to other executives at my level. One narrative I have come across a number of times is seller's remorse. This is where one person has instigated the sale of a firm that they've built or that was built by a previous generation and then felt horrible about it. Yes, they've extracted some of the value from a business that may have been around for decades, but their sense of purpose is gone, and so is all the future value they might have created. They already have an inkling that while once this firm may have done something good for society, now it is being driven hard to extract the profits that attracted the buyer in the first place.

There are times in a company's life cycle when transitioning to a PhilCo might not seem like the best option – if, say, the business is at a highly capital-intensive stage, where it might make most sense to focus on raising the investment it urgently needs. All I'd say to that is that with the most significant decisions, it will never seem like quite the right time. My advice would be to start putting the groundwork in place now. Because ultimately, there's no time like the present.

GLOSSARY

B-Corp A business that has been certified as meeting certain standards of social and environmental performance to balance profit and purpose.

Big Give A UK-based charity that provides a platform where charitable donations can be doubled through online match-funding campaigns.

Big Give's Christmas Challenge A major charity fundraising campaign in the UK.

Bluewashing A term used to describe deceptive marketing that overstates a company's commitment to responsible social practices.

Co-members A term used to refer to colleagues or employees within a company, emphasising a sense of community and shared purpose.

CSR (Corporate Social Responsibility) The practices and policies undertaken by businesses to have a positive impact on society.

Donor-advised fund (DAF) A large charitable organisation that acts as an umbrella for smaller organisations or individual philanthropists, allowing donors to specify which causes they want to support.

Edelman Trust Barometer An annual survey that measures the UK public's trust in institutions such as government, media and business.

Equity-based remuneration A compensation structure where employees receive shares or stock options as part of their pay.

ESG (Environmental, Social and Governance) A set of criteria used to evaluate a company's operations and performance in these three areas.

Foundation company A non-profit organisation or charitable trust established by a business to engage in philanthropic activities and contribute to social impact, while also potentially holding ownership or control of a business.

Free-market capitalism An economic system where prices for goods and services are determined by forces of supply and demand, with minimal government intervention.

Gift Aid A UK tax incentive that allows charities to reclaim tax on donations made by UK taxpayers, increasing the total funds received.

Golden share A type of share that gives its holder veto power over changes to a company's charter.

Greenwashing Misleading claims about the environmental benefits of a product, service or company's practices.

Hyper-capitalism An extreme form of capitalism characterised by the dominance of large organisations and the prioritisation of profit over social and environmental concerns.

Income statement Also known as a profit and loss (P&L) statement, an income statement is a financial report that shows a company's revenue, expenses, gains and losses over a specific period.

Karma capitalism A new variant of capitalism that embraces societal needs and incorporates philanthropy into business models.

LTIP (long-term incentive plan) A company policy designed to reward employees, typically executives, for achieving specific goals that enhance shareholder value over an extended period.

Match funding A fundraising strategy where donations are matched by another donor, effectively doubling the contribution.

PhilCo (Philanthropy Company) A company that has at least 10 per cent of its shares held by a charitable foundation.

Pinkwashing Exploiting LGBTQ+ advocacy for commercial gain without genuine support.

Pre-emptive rights Rights that allow existing shareholders to purchase new shares before they are offered to others, preventing dilution of their ownership.

Shareholder primacy The principle that shareholders' interests should be the primary concern of a company's management.

Social washing Misleading claims about social responsibility.

Sports washing A state or organisation using sports (hosting events, owning teams) to improve its reputation and distract from negative actions and behaviours.

Steward company A company structure where the business is legally bound to a mission, often involving social or environmental goals, and cannot be sold for profit.

Vulture capitalism A term used to describe aggressive and often unethical business practices focused solely on profit.

Whitewashing Deliberately attempting to conceal crimes or scandals.

APPENDIX

Organisations that can help

Association of Charitable Foundations www.acf.org.uk

Association of Chief Executives of Voluntary Organisations (ACEVO) www.acevo.org.uk

Big Give https://donate.biggive.org/

Charities Aid Foundation (CAF) www.cafonline.org

Charity Commission for England and Wales https://www.gov.uk/government/organisations/charity-commission

GOV.UK. *Set up a charity* https://www.gov.uk/setting-up-charity

National Council for Voluntary Organisations www.ncvo-vol.org.uk

Office of the Scottish Charity Register www.oscr.org.uk

OpenGrants. *How to start a charity or foundation: A step-by-step guide* https://opengrants.io/how-to-start-a-charity-or-foundation-a-step-by-step-guide/

Purpose https://purpose-economy.org/en/

More Information

Karma Capitalism www.karmacapitalism.org

PhilCo www.philco.org.uk

REFERENCES

Introduction

Charities Aid Foundation (2024). 'Charities struggle to meet growing demand amid financial strain'. Retrieved from https://www.cafonline. org/home/about-us/press-office/charities-struggle-to-meet-growing-demand-amid-financial-strain

Reed (n.d.). 'Reed takes home Management Today award for response to Covid-19'. Retrieved from https://www.reed.com/articles/reed-takes-home-management-today-award-for-response-to-covid-19

Chapter One

Aguilera, R. V. (2019). 'The corporate governance logic of the UN Sustainable Development Goals'. *Corporate Governance: An International Review*, 27(1), 79.

Bosch. (n.d.). 'Ownership structure and organization'. Retrieved from https://www.bosch.co.uk/our-company/bosch-group-worldwide/

Bottge, D. (2021). 'The foundation-owned company model: The path to build tomorrow's society by unifying long-termism and philanthropic impact'. University of Geneva. Retrieved from https://www.unige.ch/philanthropie/application/files/5116/1485/3060/2021-01_DB_The_foundation-owned_company_model.pdf.

Bottge, D. (2022). 'Holding foundations in Switzerland: The foundation-owned company model from theory to practice'. University of Geneva. Retrieved from https://www.unige.ch/philanthropie/application/files/3416/7145/5413/Slatkine_Holding_Foundations_DB_Dec_2022.pdf

Butler, P. (2022). 'Millions forced to skip meals as UK cost of living crisis deepens'. *Guardian*. Retrieved from https://www.theguardian.com/society/2022/oct/18/millions-forced-to-skip-meals-as-uk-cost-of-living-crisis-deepens

Carlsberg Group. (n.d.). 'Shareholders'. Retrieved from https://www.carlsberggroup.com/investor-relations/shareholders/

Charities Aid Foundation. (2024). 'Charities Struggle to Meet Growing Demand Amid Financial Strain'. Retrieved from https://www.cafon line.org/home/about-us/press-office/charities-struggle-to-meet-growing-demand-amid-financial-strain

Charities Aid Foundation. (2024). 'Charity Resilience Index'. Retrieved from https://www.cafonline.org/insights/research/charity-resilience-index

Hansmann, H., and Thomsen, S. (2021). 'The governance of foundation-owned firms'. *Journal of Legal Analysis, 13*(1), 172–230.

INGKA Foundation. (n.d.). 'Ownership of INGKA Group'. Retrieved from https://www.ingkafoundation.org/ownership-of-ingka-group/

LEGO Group. (n.d.). 'About us: The LEGO Group'. Retrieved from https://www.lego.com/en-gb/aboutus/lego-group?locale=en-gb

Millenary Watches. (n.d.). 'Who owns Rolex? Here's the answer!' Retrieved from https://millenarywatches.com/who-owns-rolex/

The Equality Trust. 'The scale of economic inequality in the UK'. The Equality Trust. Retrieved from https://equalitytrust.org.uk/scale-economic-inequality-uk/

Thomsen, S., and Kavadis, N. (2022). 'Enterprise foundations: Law, taxation, governance, and performance'. *Annals of Corporate Governance, 6*(4), 227–333.

Thomsen, S., Poulsen, T., Børsting, C., and Kuhn, J. (2021). 'Foundation ownership and firm performance: Evidence from a large international sample'. *Corporate Governance: An International Review, 29*(6), 525–543.

Chapter Two

Barnardo's. (2024). 'Changing childhoods, changing lives'. Retrieved from https://www.barnardos.org.uk/sites/default/files/2024-03/Changing%20Childhoods%20Changing%20Lives%20report.pdf

Charities Aid Foundation (2023). 'Corporate giving by the FTSE 100'. Retrieved from corporate-giving-by-ftse-100-report-2023.pdf

Founders Pledge (2025). Retrieved from https://www.founders
pledge.com

The Giving Pledge (2025). Retrieved from https://givingpledge.org

Harbert, T. (2019). 'Here's how much the 2008 bailouts really cost'.
Retrieved from https://mitsloan.mit.edu/ideas-made-to-matter/heres-
how-much-2008-bailouts-really-cost

Laville, S. and A. Leach (2022). 'Water companies' debts since
privatisation: Ofwat refuses to impose limits'. *Guardian*. Retrieved
from https://www.theguardian.com/environment/2022/dec/01/
water-companies-debts-since-privatisation-ofwat-refuses-impose-limits

Lucas. J. (2025). 'Trust in business is built on action, not just words'.
Edelman. Retrieved from https://www.edelman.co.uk/research/trust-
business-built-action-not-just-words

May, M. (2023). 'Charitable giving by FTSE 100 companies drops
a quarter in a decade'. Retrieved from https://fundraising.
co.uk/2023/07/17/charitable-giving-by-ftse-100-companies-drops-a-
quarter-in-a-decade-research-suggests/

McKinsey & Company (2020). 'From there to here: 50 years of
thinking on the social responsibility of business'. Retrieved from
https://www.mckinsey.com/featured-insights/corporate-purpose/
from-there-to-here-50-years-of-thinking-on-the-social-responsibility-
of-business

National Philanthropic Trust (2023). 'Charitable giving statistics'.
Retrieved from https://www.nptrust.org/philanthropic-resources/
charitable-giving-statistics/

Norman, S. (2025). 'Lloyds Bank urged to release full HBOS review'.
City A.M. Retrieved from https://www.cityam.com/lloyds-urged-to-
release-full-hbos-review/

Stempel, J. (2023). 'Warren Buffett's charitable giving tops $51 billion'.
Retrieved from https://www.reuters.com/markets/us/warren-
buffetts-charitable-giving-tops-51-billion-2023-06-22/

Topf, A. (10 October 2014). 'The 10 biggest energy company
bankruptcies'. Retrieved from https://oilprice.com/Energy/Energy-
General/The-10-Biggest-Energy-Company-Bankruptcies.html

Chapter Three

Bivens, J., E. Gould, and J. Kandra (2024). 'CEO pay declined in 2023'. Economic Policy Institute. Retrieved from https://www.epi.org/publication/ceo-pay-in-2023/

Charities Aid Foundation (2024). 'Charities Struggle to Meet Growing Demand Amid Financial Strain'. Retrieved from https://www.cafonline.org/home/about-us/press-office/charities-struggle-to-meet-growing-demand-amid-financial-strain

Ferrell-Schweppenstedde, D. (2025). 'Challenges and opportunities facing the charity sector'. Charities Aid Foundation. Retrieved from https://www.cafonline.org/about-us/blog-home/charities-blog/challenges-and-opportunties-facing-charity-sector

Gibbons, S. & C. A. L. Hilber (2023). 'Charity in the time of austerity: In search of the "Big Society"'. Centre for Economic Performance. Retrieved from https://cep.lse.ac.uk/_NEW/publications/abstract.asp?index=9616

The Health Foundation (2024). 'In-work poverty trends'. Retrieved from https://www.health.org.uk/evidence-hub/money-and-resources/poverty/in-work-poverty-trends

Hemming, R., and J. A. Kay (1980). 'The Laffer Curve'. *Fiscal Studies*, 1(2), 83–90.

HM Treasury. (2025). 'Public spending statistics release: February 2025'. Retrieved from https://www.gov.uk/government/statistics/public-spending-statistics-release-february-2025

New Economics Foundation (2023). 'New analysis shows £22bn in hidden cuts to public services in today's budget'. Retrieved from https://neweconomics.org/2023/03/new-analysis-shows-22bn-in-hidden-cuts-to-public-services-in-todays-budget#:~:text=New%20analysis%20of%20today%27s%20Spring,New%20Economics%20Foundation%20(NEF)

Qureshi, Z. (2023). 'Rising inequality: A major issue of our time'. Brookings Institution. Retrieved from https://www.brookings.edu/articles/rising-inequality-a-major-issue-of-our-time/

United Nations (2023). '9.7 billion on Earth by 2050, growth rate slowing, says new UN population report'. Retrieved from https://www. un.org/en/academic-impact/97-billion-earth-2050-growth-rate-slowing-says-new-un-population-report

United Nations Environment Programme Finance Initiative (2004). 'Who cares wins: Global Compact'. Retrieved from https://www. unepfi.org/fileadmin/events/2004/stocks/who_cares_wins_global_compact_2004.pdf

Watt, N. (2010). 'David Cameron's Big Society cuts'. *Guardian*. Retrieved from https://www.theguardian.com/politics/2010/jul/19/david-cameron-big-society-cuts

Chapter Four

Akepa – The Sustainability Agency (2025). 'Greenwashing: 18 recent stand-out examples'. Retrieved from https://thesustainableagency. com/blog/greenwashing-examples/

Blake, H. (2013). 'A history of Novo Nordisk'. *Pharmaphorum*. Retrieved from https://pharmaphorum.com/views-and-analysis/a_history_of-_novo_nordisk

Christensen, C. M., T. Hall, K. Dillon, and D. S. Duncan (2016). 'Know your customers' "jobs to be done"'. *Harvard Business Review*. Retrieved from https://hbr.org/2016/09/know-your-customers-jobs-to-be-done

Daly, L. (2025). 'What is greenwashing?'. *The Motley Fool*. Retrieved from https://www.fool.com/investing/stock-market/types-of-stocks/esg-investing/greenwashing-examples/

Greenfield, P. (2023). 'Revealed: Forest carbon offsets biggest provider worthless, Verra AOE'. *Guardian*. Retrieved from https://www. theguardian.com/environment/2023/jan/18/revealed-forest-carbon-offsets-biggest-provider-worthless-verra-aoe

Ho, V. (2023). 'The discrimination pushing LGBTQ workers to quit'. *BBC Worklife*. Retrieved from https://www.bbc.com/worklife/article/20230303-the-discrimination-pushing-lgbtq-workers-to-quit

Hotton, R. (2015). 'Volkswagen: The scandal explained'. *BBC News*. Retrieved from https://www.bbc.co.uk/news/business-34324772

Lawson, A., and H. Horton (2023). 'Ban bonuses to water company bosses, Ofwat told'. *Guardian*. Retrieved from https://www.theguardian.com/business/2023/nov/08/water-company-bosses-bonuses-ofwat

Levingston, I. (2025). 'Raspberry Pi soars on debut in boost for London IPO market'. *Financial Times*. Retrieved from https://www.ft.com/content/69324884-a626-4787-a4ce-aece410d1dcc

Reuters (2020). 'Volkswagen says diesel scandal has cost it 31.3 billion euros'. *Reuters*. Retrieved from https://www.reuters.com/article/business/volkswagen-says-diesel-scandal-has-cost-it-313-billion-euros-idUSKBN2141JA/

Schlicht, G. A. (2022). 'Reflecting on the UN Global Compact: What went wrong?' *LSE Business Review*. Retrieved from https://blogs.lse.ac.uk/businessreview/2022/07/26/reflecting-on-the-un-global-compact-what-went-wrong/

Topham, G. (2022). 'BP accused of using social media influencers to greenwash image amid calls for windfall tax'. *Guardian*. Retrieved from https://www.theguardian.com/business/2022/aug/06/bp-social-media-influence-ads-labour-windfall-tax

UN Global Compact. 'Participation'. Retrieved from https://unglobalcompact.org/participation

Chapter Five

Ballou, B. (2023). 'When private equity firms bankrupt their own companies'. *The Atlantic*. Retrieved from https://www.theatlantic.com/ideas/archive/2023/05/private-equity-firms-bankruptcies-plunder-book/673896/#

Bottge, D. (2021). 'The foundation-owned Company model: The path to build tomorrow's society by unifying long-termism and philanthropic impact'. University of Geneva. Retrieved from https://www.unige.ch/philanthropie/application/files/5116/1485/3060/2021-01_DB_The_foundation-owned_company_model.pdf.

Bradley, C. 'What happened to the world's "greatest" companies?' McKinsey & Company. Retrieved from https://www.mckinsey.com/capabilities/strategy-and-corporate-finance/our-insights/the-strategy-and-corporate-finance-blog/what-happened-to-the-worlds-greatest-companies

Collins, J. (2001). *Good to Great: Why Some Companies Make the Leap . . . and Others Don't*. HarperBusiness.

Collins, J., and J. I. Porras (1994). *Built to Last: Successful Habits of Visionary Companies*. HarperBusiness.

Hansmann, H., and S. Thomsen (2021). 'The governance of foundation-owned firms'. *Journal of Legal Analysis, 13*(1), 172–230.

Hill, A. L. Mellon, and J. Goddard (2018). 'How winning organizations last 100 years'. *Harvard Business Review*. Retrieved from https://hbr. org/2018/09/how-winning-organizations-last-100-years

Peters, T. J., and R. H. Waterman (1982). *In Search of Excellence: Lessons from America's Best-Run Companies*. Harper & Row.

Schroeder, D., and S. Thomson (2019). 'Foundation ownership and sustainability international evidence'. *European Corporate Governance Institute*. Retrieved from https://www.ecgi.global/sites/default/files/Paper:%20David%20Schroeder,%20Steen%20Thomsen.pdf

Statista. 'Average company lifespan'. Retrieved from https://www.statista.com/statistics/1259275/average-company-lifespan/

Thomsen, S., T. Poulsen, C. Børsting, and J. Kuhn (2018). 'Industrial foundations as long-term owners'. *Corporate Governance: An International Review, 26*, 180–196.

Chapter Six

A. P. Moller Foundation (n.d.). 'About the A. P. Moller and Chastine Mc-Kinney Moller Foundation'. Retrieved from https://www.apmollerfonde.dk/the-a-p-moller-foundation/

AbodeHR (n.d.). 'What you need to recruit and retain Gen Z'. Retrieved from https://www.abodehr.com/blog/what-you-need-to-recruit-and-retain-gen-z#:~:text=The%20Current%20State%20Of%20Gen,grads%20in%202023%20than%202022

Beevers, A. (2023). 'People are at the heart of our business, says IKEA'. *The Retail Bulletin*. Retrieved from https://www.theretail

bulletin.com/home-and-diy/people-are-at-the-heart-of-our-business-says-ikea-09-02-2023/

Bill & Melinda Gates Foundation. (n.d.). 'Our story'. Retrieved from https://www.gatesfoundation.org/about/our-story

Børsting, C., and S. Thomsen (2018). 'Foundation ownership, reputation, and labour'. *Oxford Review of Economic Policy*. Retrieved from https://ssrn.com/abstract=2955572

Davis. J. (2017). How Lego clicked: The super brand that reinvented itself. *Guardian*. Retrieved from https://www.theguardian.com/lifeandstyle/2017/jun/04/how-lego-clicked-the-super-brand-that-reinvented-itself

De Smet, A., M. Mugayar-Baldocchi, A. Reich, and B. Schaninger. 'Some employees are destroying value, others are building it'. McKinsey & Company. Retrieved from https://www.mckinsey.com/capabilities/people-and-organizational-performance/our-insights/some-employees-are-destroying-value-others-are-building-it-do-you-know-the-difference

Ecosia. (n.d.). 'Ecosia – the search engine that plants trees'. Retrieved from https://www.ecosia.org/

IKEA Global. (n.d.). 'Our culture and values'. Retrieved from https://www.ikea.com/global/en/our-business/how-we-work/ikea-culture-and-values/

Maersk. (2024). 'Human capital'. Retrieved from https://investor.maersk.com/static-files/31bf05a1-6f0c-4fbd-a3c7-3f58e044f668

Matthews, C. M. (2024). 'Inside the Rockefeller clan's intensifying feud with Exxon'. *Wall Street Journal*. Retrieved from https://www.tovima.com/wsj/inside-the-rockefeller-clans-intensifying-feud-with-exxon/

New Policy Institute (n.d.). 'Beyond shareholder value'. Retrieved from https://www.npi.org.uk/files/3814/0482/3043/Beyond_Shareholder_Value_FINAL.pdf

Philanthropy Roundtable (n.d.). 'Andrew Carnegie'. Retrieved from https://www.philanthropyroundtable.org/hall-of-fame/andrew-carnegie/

Purpose Economy. (n.d.). 'BuurtzorgT case study'. Retrieved from https://purpose-economy.org/content/uploads/purpose-bzt-case study.pdf

Robertson, D., and B. Breen (2014). *Brick by Brick: How Lego Rewrote the Rules of Innovation and Conquered the Global Toy Industry*. Random House.

Segal. M. (2022). 'IKEA Foundation to deploy $600 million in climate funding'. *ESG Today*. Retrieved from https://www.esgtoday.com/ikea-foundation-to-deploy-600-million-in-climate-funding/

Thomsen, S., T. Poulsen, C. Børsting, and J. Kuhn (2018). 'Industrial foundations as long-term owners'. *Corporate Governance: An International Review*, 26, 180–196.

Workplace.com (n.d.). 'Gen Z in the workplace'. Retrieved from https://thoughtexchange.com/guide/gen-z-at-work/

Chapter Seven

GlassOnline. (2024). 'Carl Zeiss Foundation celebrates 125 years with speech by Chancellor'. Retrieved from https://www.glassonline.com/carl-zeiss-foundation-celebrates-125-years-with-speech-by-chancellor/

King, I. (2024). 'Raspberry Pi soars on debut in boost for London IPO market'. *Sky News*. Retrieved from https://news.sky.com/story/raspberry-pi-soars-on-debut-in-boost-for-london-ipo-market-13151122

Patagonia (2022). 'Patagonia's next chapter: Earth is now our only shareholder'. Retrieved from https://www.patagoniaworks.com/press/2022/9/14/patagonias-next-chapter-earth-is-now-our-only-shareholder

Raspberry Pi (2024). 'Raspberry Pi IPO'. Retrieved from https://www.raspberrypi.com/news/raspberry-pi-ipo/

Reed Foundation (2023). 'Annual accounts'. Retrieved from https://register-of-charities.charitycommission.gov.uk/en/charity-search/-/charity-details/264728/accounts-and-annual-returns

Robert Bosch Stiftung (2024). 'Annual report 2023'. Retrieved from https://www.bosch-stiftung.de/en/annual-report-2023

Chapter Eight

Milken Institute (2023). 'Corporate philanthropy: Emerging strategies for lasting impact'. Retrieved from https://milkeninstitute.org/content-hub/research-and-reports/reports/corporate-philanthropy-emerging-strategies-lasting-impact

Novo Nordisk Foundation (n.d.). 'Frontpage – Novo Nordisk Fonden'. Retrieved from https://novonordiskfonden.dk/en/

Palazzo, G., & U. Richter (2005). 'Business as usual? The case of the tobacco industry'. *Journal of Business Ethics, 61*(4), 387–401.

Philip Morris International (2018). 'Giving back, wherever we are'. Retrieved from https://www.pmi.com/sustainability/integrated-report-2018/community/giving-back-wherever-we-are

Philip Morris International (2020). '2020 social contributions at a glance'. Retrieved from https://www.pmi.com/resources/docs/default-source/pmi-sustainability/2020-social-contributions.pdf?sfvrsn=2fdd6eb7_2

Strategic Philanthropy Inc. (n.d.). 'Best practices of corporate philanthropy – What's the right amount of money to give to charities?' Retrieved from https://strategicphilanthropyinc.com/best-practices-of-corporate-philanthropy-whats-the-right-amount-of-money-to-give-to-charities/

Chapter Nine

1% for the Planet (n.d.). '1% for the Planet'. Retrieved from https://www.onepercentfortheplanet.org/

Big Give (n.d.). 'Match funding research report launched'. Retrieved from https://biggive.org/match-funding-research-report-launched

Patagonia (2022). 'Patagonia's next chapter: Earth is now our only shareholder'. Patagonia Works. Retrieved from https://www.

patagoniaworks.com/press/2022/9/14/patagonias-next-chapter-earth-is-now-our-only-shareholder

Womankind Worldwide (2025). 'Home – Womankind Worldwide'. Retrieved from https://www.womankind.org.uk/

Chapter Ten

Edelman (2023). '2023 Edelman Trust Barometer'. Retrieved from https://www.edelman.com/news-awards/2023-edelman-trust-barometer

ACKNOWLEDGEMENTS

I would like to thank Teena Lyons, who did the lion's share of the heavy lifting on this project, and Tim de Lisle, who helped me to edit the original manuscript and improved it by doing so. Additional thanks should go to my team, Ellen D'Amico, Katie Johns and Chris Legge, who helped with the research, and to Alex Day and Jen May, who brought PhilCo business leaders together to share their experiences and ideas.

Thanks are due too to John Townsend and Darren Burnett for their contribution to the design of the book. I am glad that you encouraged me to use pictures as well as words. Thank you to my son, Harry Reed, for the supplementary photography, to Stefan Gatt for his photographs of my rescue from the Matterhorn and to Michael Woods for the photograph of the author.

And a big thank you to my publisher, Elizabeth Bond, to my editor, Fionn Hargreaves, and the team at Ebury. Your belief in this project has been unwavering and your guidance invaluable.

There are so many people I have worked with over the years who have contributed to my learning; every day and every conversation brings new lessons. I would like to thank everyone past and present that I have worked with at Reed and, earlier in my career, elsewhere.

Lastly, I would like to thank my wonderful wife, Nicola, for constantly encouraging me to share these ideas and for reading and improving the early drafts.

Wishing all readers good karma. It's time to spread the word.

INDEX

Page references in *italics* indicate images.

Abbe, Ernst 151, 153
academy schools 45
ageing population/population
    collapse 54–5
Alec Reed Academy 25
Amoco 91
Andrews Property Group 151
Anheuser-Busch 151
Annual Report 67–72, *69, 72, 75, 78,*
    81, 82
AP Moller 115
Arts Council 58
Arts for Impact appeal (Big Give)
    180, 181
Asea Brown Boveri (ABB) 92
ask, the (amount of money a
    charity seeks from
    individuals) 177, 178
asset stripping 43–4
Auditors' Report 71
Aurelius 101
austerity programmes 60

B-Corps 20
Bank of Scotland 43
BBC 92
Bengal, India 41
Berkshire Hathaway 46
Berners-Lee, Tim 197, 198
Big Donors 178
Big Give 9, 62, 179–89, 208, 213
    Arts for Impact appeal
        180, 181
    attracting talent and 117
    campaigns, number of per year
        180–1
    Champions 179–81, 185, 186

Christmas Challenge 127–8, 181,
    189, 207, 213
co-members and 188–9
Covid-related charity appeals and 35
diversity of causes 186
double-matching principle and 181
Gift Aid and 180
goals, fundraising 19, 182
Green Match Fund 180
Grenfell Tower campaign 25
lessons from 185–6
match-funding and 19, 20, 25, 179
origins 25, 179–80
PhilTech and 20
Pledgers 179–81
1:1, or Pledge Model and 179
stakeholders, engagement of
    188–9
third-sector organisation, not a
    model that works for every
    186
£350 million raised by 19
trustees 167
unrestricted funds 182
winter appeal 184
Big Hairy Audacious Goals (BHAGs)
    94
Big Society 60
Bill & Melinda Gates Foundation
    122
Blok, Jos de 128
Bloody Good Period 162–3, *162*
bluewashing 79, 213
Body Shop, The 99, 101
Bosch 20, 139–41, 154, 205, 208
Bosch, Robert 139–41, 205, 208
Bournville village 41, *96*

brand, strengthening 109–31
  employee engagement 112–16
  foundation-owned companies'
    survival after 40 years *126*
  IKEA and 113, 114, 115
  innovation/Lego 124–6
  legacy 121–3
  long-service celebrations 111–12
  Maersk and 115
  original values become integral
    part of Philco 123–4
  PhilCo ownership and 113
  quiet quitters 113
  resilience 126–30, *128, 129*
  satisfaction, charity-giving and
    130–1
  talent, attracting 117–21
Brick by Brick: How Lego Rewrote
  the Rules of Innovation and
  Conquered the Global
  Toy Industry
  (Green/Robertson) 125
Briscoe, Lisa 57–9, *57*
Buffett, Warren 46
building societies 20
  deregulation of 42
business
  books on 91–4
  capitalism and *see* capitalism
  cyclical nature of 35
  Environmental, Social and
    Governance (ESG) and
    see Environmental, Social
    and Governance (ESG)
  giving business 45–9
  lifespan of, average 91
  positive view of, creating a more
    201–2
  purpose of 33–49, 195–8
  shareholders/shares and
    see shareholders/shares
  social responsibility and *see* social
    responsibility

  trust in 47, 49
BuurtzorgT 128, 129–30, *129*

Cadbury 41, *96*
Cadbury, George 96
Cameron, David 60
capitalism
  abuses of power and 42–4
  asset stripping 43–4
  Britain, origins in 38–41
  building societies, deregulation of
    42–3
  business and *see* business
  charitable contributions, reduction
    in and 34, 36–8
  DNA of 12, 20–21, 202
  financial crisis (2008–9) and 24,
    42–3, 45, 59, 126, 202
  free-market capitalism 21, 45,
    49, 214
  hyper-capitalism, dangers of
    38–45, 214
  Karma capitalism *see* Karma
    capitalism
  profits, rise in and 34, 36–8
  reform of/need for different kind
    of 21, 84–5, 195, 198
  shareholder primacy 21, 41–2, 67,
    137, 164, 195, 196, 198, 215
  short-term profits, focus on 21,
    37, 41, 97, 98–101, 125, 138,
    139, 154
  vulture capitalism 25, 215
  woke capitalism 195
carbon emissions 76, 77, 80, 83, 85
  net zero 77, 79
Cardboard Citizens 57–9, *57*
career defining moment 3–9
Carl Zeiss Foundation 151, 153
Carlsberg 20, 123–4, 151
Carlsberg Foundation 124
Carnegie, Andrew 122
Cath Kidston 99

Chairman's Report 71
Chapman, Alexandra 167
charitable foundations 157–70
   brand identity and 165
   Charity Commission and 159,
      165–6, 168, 169
   PhilCo models and 142, 145
   PhilCo status and 19, 20, 103, 111,
      165, 205, 207
   purpose of 159–64
   setting up 139–40
   spending proceeds of corporate
      philanthropy 161, 171–89
   trustees 165–8
Charity Commission 149–50, 159,
   165, 166, 168, 206
charity sector 51–64
   charitable foundations *see*
      charitable foundations
   cost-of-giving crisis / competitive
      environment within 34,
      36–8, 183
   Covid-19 and *see* Covid-19
   demand for, rising 53
   ESG and *see* Environmental,
      Social and Governance
      activity
   inequality and 53–5, 54
   moral obligation to donate 122
   religion, decline in popularity of
      organised and 37–8
   state support and 56–64
   See also individual charity name
Chief Executive's Report 71
Chouinard, Malinda 173–4
Chouinard, Yvon 153–4, 173–4
Christensen, Clayton 75
Christiansen, Ole Kirk 124–5
Circuit City 91
City of London 39–40
climate change 57, 70, 75, 76, 78,
   79, 82, 84, 118, 120, 121,
   139, 196

coalition government (2010–2015)
   59–60
Cohen, Professor Lauren 3, 121
Colligan, Philip 148–50
Collins, Jim
   Built to Last (with Jerry Porras)
      91, 94
   Good to Great 91
Companies Act (2006) 70, 71
company lifespan, average 91, 99
cost-of-giving crisis 183
cost-of-living crisis 21, 23, 57, 183
Covid-19 pandemic 21, 24, 35–6, 59,
   183, 184
Crazy Ways for Crazy Days (TV
   programme) 92
CSR (Corporate Social
   Responsibility) 37, 62, 213

Data General 91
DEC 91
Dee Group 11, 143
Deep Mind 46
Denmark 98, 103, 115, 123, 124, 126,
   161, 200, 202
Dent du Géant mountains 4
Disasters Emergency Committee 182
donor-advised fund (DAF) 169, 213
double foundation 153–5
double-matching principle 181

East India Company 41
Ecosia 118–21
Edelman Trust Barometer 47,
   196, 213
Enron 43
Environmental, Social and
   Governance (ESG) 65–85, 214
   accountability, lack of 75–7
   Annual Report and 67–71, 75, 78,
      81, 82
   bluewashing 79, 213
   defined 68

Environmental, Social and
    Governance (ESG) – *cont.*
eclipses charitable giving 81–2
greenwashing 78, 79, 163, 164, 214
growth of 68–73
immediacy, lack of 76–8
incomplete or selective
    reporting 74
insufficient integration into core
    business practices 75
meaningless virtue signalling, or
    boxticking exercises 73–4
misleading, purposefully 78
origins 67–8
pinkwashing 80, 215
Principles for Responsible
    Investment (PRI) 67
regulation and standardisation,
    lack of 74
social washing 78, 80, 215
UN Sustainable Development
    Goals and 70
whitewashing 80–1, 215
woke capitalism and 195
Ethiopiaid 25, 175
EU Taxonomy for sustainable
    activities 70

FareShare South West 182–4, *182*
financial reports 67–71, 75, 78, 81,
    82, 206, 214
Flower Pod 188
Forsyth, Josie 182–4, *182*
Founders Pledge 46
Frankel (racehorse) 28
free-market capitalism 21, 45,
    49, 214
Friedman, Milton 37, 42, 46, 112,
    195, 196
FTSE 100 36, 68–9, 71, 74, 91

Galileo 28
Gates, Bill 122

Gatt, Stefan 4, 231
Gen Z 113, 117, 205
Gift Aid 146, 169, 180, 214
Gillette 91
Giving Pledge 46
Giving Tuesday 181
global financial crisis (2008–9) 24,
    42–3, 45, 59, 126, 202
Golden Share 129, 156, 214
Google 118
Green Match Fund 180
greenwashing 78, 79, 163, 164, 214
Grenfell Tower fire (2017) 25
Grocott, Rachel 162–3, *162*
Guardian Media Group 151

Halifax Bank of Scotland
    (HBOS) 43
Halifax Permanent Benefit Building
    Society 42–3
Harvard University 75
    Business School 3, 92, 121
Help the Aged 174
Hill Samuel 10, 11, 143
HMP Holloway 175
Holdfast Collective 154

IKEA 20, 113, 114, 115
income statement 68–9, *69*, 214
Indonesian Tsunami Appeal 181
Industrial Revolution 41
inequality 41, 53–5, 196
INGKA Foundation 113, 114, 115
Initial Public Offering (IPO) 147,
    149, 150, 201
innovation 21, 47, 93, 94, 118, 124,
    125–6, 129, 137, 202
investment funds, international 43
in-work poverty 53–4

Jacobsen, Jacob Christian 123–4
John Lewis 20
joint-stock company 38–9, 41, 43, 45

Kabbage 46
Karma capitalism 195
 defined 21, 214
 PhilCo status and 155, 196, 198,
  202, 211
 readiness for 25
Keep Britain Working campaign 35
Keveral Farm 127
Kmart 91
Knudstorp, Jørgen Vig 125
Kodak 91
Kroll, Christian 118–21, *119*
Kwok, Ken 9

Laffer Curve 55, *55*
Lane Group 92
Lego 20, 124–5
Lego Foundation 124–5
Level 5 leaders 94
Lever, William Hesketh 96
LGBTQ+ community 80, 84, 215
Lindt 95, 151
listed companies 146
London Stock Exchange 99
longevity, corporate 27, 89–108, 210
 backseat driving 101, 102
 Big Hairy Audacious Goals
  (BHAGs) and 93
 business books and 91–4
 foundation-owned companies
  and 96
 innovation and creativity and
  124–6, *126*
 Level 5 leaders 93
 Peters identifies eight things
  essential to 92–4
  1. A bias for action 92
  2. Close to the customer 93
  3. Autonomy and
   entrepreneurship 93
  4. Productivity through
   people 93
  5. Hands-on, value-driven 93
  6. Stick to the knitting 93
  7. Simple form, lean staff 93
  8. Simultaneous loose-tight
   properties 93
 PhilCo model and 97–105
 private equity and 99, 100, 101
 short-termism and 98–101
 Stapelstein and 106–8, *106*
 survival after 40 years, foundation-
  owned companies' *126*
 vulnerability, removing 101–5
 LTIP (long-term incentive plan)
  77, 215

Maersk 115, *132*
match-funding 19, 25, 26, 27, 181,
  185, 213
Matterhorn, Alps 3–9
McKinsey 94, 112
Medicare 10, 140, 143
Merkel, Angela 151
Microsoft 122
Middle East Humanitarian
 Disaster Appeal 181
Moleman, Nico 128, 129–30
Morrisons 99
Muscovy Company 38–9
Myanmar 181

Natura 101
net zero 77, 79
New York Times 37
non-executive directors
 (NEDs) 150
non-profit organisations 97, 141–2,
  151, 153, 154, 159, 169,
  201, 214
Novo Group 161
Novo Nordisk Foundation 103, 161

offshore, businesses registered 43
1:1 pledge model 179, 186–7
Ozempic 103, 161

Paris Agreement (2015) 76
Patagonia 153–5, 173
　'1% for the Planet' 173
　Patagonia Perpetual Ownership
　　Trust 154–5
Peters, Tom: *In Search of Excellence*
　91–4
Petralia, Kathryn 46
PhilCo, or Philanthropy Company
　9, 11, 12
　brand and brand
　charitable foundation and *see*
　　charitable foundation
　company name and 165
　company structure and 139–40
　creating 133–56
　defined 12, 17–28
　Denmark and *see* Denmark
　directors of business and trustees
　　of the charitable foundation,
　　crossover between 142
　dual purpose 97
　employee engagement
　　and 112–16
　innovation and *see* innovation
　Karma capitalism and *see* Karma
　　capitalism
　legacy and 27, 121–3, 140, 143
　listed companies and 146
　longevity and *see* longevity,
　　corporate
　model 97–8
　models, choosing 135–56
　　four models 141–56
　　　1. Minority investor – the
　　　　Reed model (10–20 per cent
　　　　shareholding) 143, 145
　　　2. Investor plus – Raspberry Pi
　　　　(20–49 per cent shareholding)
　　　　145–50, *148*
　　　3. Foundation–owned – Carl
　　　　Zeiss (100 per cent
　　　　shareholding) 151–3

　　　4. Double foundation –
　　　　Patagonia (100 per cent
　　　　shareholding) 153–5
　　commonalities between various
　　　models 155–56
　　self-governance and 155–56
　　purpose and 156
　　flexibility and 146
　notable examples, UK 98
　original values of company
　　and 123–4
　origins 137, 138–9, 151
　plug-and-play model 168–9
　profitability/commercial success
　　and 115, *128*
　questions, frequently asked 203–10
　raising capital 140–1
　resilience of 126–30, *128*
　satisfaction, personal and 130–1
　shares/shareholding and *see*
　　shares/shareholding
　spending *see* spending
　start-ups and 140–1
　survival rates 23, *126*
　talent, impact on attracting 117–18
　Tax Reform Act, US (1969)
　　and 98
　trial and error process 137
　voting rights *see* voting rights
Philip Morris 160, 162
PhilTech (Philanthropy
　Technology) 20
pinkwashing 80, 215
Piz Badile mountains 4
Pledgers 179–81
pledge model, 1:1 179, 186–7
Port Sunlight, Merseyside 95–6, *190*
poverty 21, 53–4, 57, 122, 184, 186
pre-emptive rights 170, 215
Pride month 80
Principles for Responsible
　　Investment (PRI) 67
private equity 43, 99, 100

profits
  income statement and 68, 214
  non-profit organisation 97, 141–2,
    151, 153, 154, 159, 169, 201,
    214
  Reed 24, 201
  relentless pursuit of 21, 41–2, 46,
    97, 112, 137, 139, 195, 215
  rise in corporate 34, 36–8
public expenditure, UK 59
public services 45, 55, 60, 199
Purpose Evergreen Capital 105, 129
Purpose Foundation 107, 120, 129,
  208
Purpose Ventures 105

questions, frequently asked (FAQs)
  203–10
  How much will it cost me? 208
  I want to start a PhilCo. Where do
    I begin? 205
  I work for a business – how do I
    persuade my boss to do
    this? 210
  If you can't sell a PhilCo, what
    happens when the founder
    gets tired, loses interest or is
    unable to work? 209
  Is it just another way of skinning
    the ESG cat? 206–7
  Why not employee ownership?
    205–6
  Wouldn't lots of companies
    already consider themselves to
    be PhilCos? 207–8

Raspberry Pi 140, 146–50, 148, 201
Raspberry Pi Foundation 140,
  146–50, 148, 169, 201
Raychem 91
Reach Learning Disability 61–2, 61,
  187–8, 187
recession, economic 10, 24, 35

Reed/Reed Group 3
  Annual Reports 71–2, 72
  bonuses, co-member 113
  co-members work for charity
    one day a week 22, 23, 27,
    145, 149, 188, 192
  commercial success and PhilCo
    structure 115, 117, 199–200
  Covid-19 pandemic and 35
  destination employer 23
  ESG reporting 71–2, 72
  frugality 129
  long-service celebration
    lunches 111
  loyalty to co-members 127
  origins of 19
  PhilCo status 9, 11–12, 19–27, 95,
    117, 123, 143–5, 155, 161–8,
    173, 174–82, 189, 197, 199–200
  profit before tax since 1985 24
  Reed.ai 196–8
  reed.co.uk 196
  Reed Foundation ownership, 18
    per cent 19, 23, 27, 102, 142,
    145, 155
  resilience 124–8, 126
  sabbaticals 111
  talent recruitment 117–21
  trust culture within 189
Reed, Adrianne 10, 143
Reed, Sir Alec v, 92
  cancer diagnosis 9–11
  Keveral Farm and 127
  ninetieth birthday 131
  PhilCo status, on Reed's 199–200
  Reed Charity origins and 9–11
  Reed Employment, opens first
    office of 19
  Reed Foundation and 24, 25, 137,
    140, 143, 164, 167, 174–8,
    179, 197
Reed Business School 25
Reed Charity 11, 143

Reed Executive 11, 140
Reed Foundation
  Big Donors and 178–9
  Big Give and *see* Big Give
  charitable objectives 164
  leadership teams 175
  match funding 18–80
  minority-investor model and 143,
    145–6
  model, origins of 174–9
  origins 19, 137, 140, 143, 145, 164,
    175–6
  predatory takeovers and 102
  Reed Global administrative
    support for 145
  Reed Group company name
    and 165
  Reed Group strategy and 161
  shares in Reed Group, 18 per cent
    ownership 19, 23, 27, 102,
    142, 145
  shares in Reed Group, first
    acquires 142
  social entrepreneur 24–5
  trustees 165–8
  UK Youth, £1 million grant
    made to 130–3
Reed Global 145
Reed, Harry 3–6
Reed, Nicola 7–9
Reed Restart 175
Reed, Taba 28
renumeration 70, 149
  equity-based 149, 213
  executive pay 37, 68, 75
  trustee 150
resilience 126–30, *128*
Roberta (Italian mountain
  rescue crew) 7, 12
Robson, Mike 178
Rockefeller, John D. 122
Roddick, Anita 99, 101
Rohingya Refugee Crisis Appeal 181

Rolex 20, 123
RP Ltd 146

salary 37, 70, 117–18, 149, *153*
Sandhu, Julia 17–8, *187*
satisfaction, charity giving and
  personal 130–1
Schenk, Stephan 105–8
self-steering strategy 130
shares/shareholders
  building-society deregulation
    and 43, 44
  corporate donations, decline in
    and 37
  donating shares 168–70
  employee share option schemes
    120, 209
  ESG criteria and 68, 195, 196
  family members, selling to 138
  Golden Share 129, 156, 214
  joint-stock company and
    38–9, 41
  LTIP (long-term incentive plan
    share awards) 76, 215
  managers, selling to 138
  PhilCo models and 20, 27, 97,
    101–105, 107, 121, 122, 129,
    141–6, 159, 207, 209
  pre-emptive rights 215
  Reed Group and *see* Reed Group
  shareholder primacy 21, 41–2, 67,
    137, 164, 195, 196, 198, 215
Shatwell, Stephen 61–2, *61*
short-termism 21, 37, 41, 97,
  98–101, 125, 138, 139, 154
social washing 78, 80, 215
S172 Statement (Section 172 of the
  Companies Act 2006) 70–1
spending proceeds of corporate
  philanthropy 161, 171–89
  ask, the 177, 188
  Big Give and 179–82, 185–7
  co-members and 188–9

FareShare South West and
182–4, *182*
match funding and 178–9, 181
Reach Learning Disability and
187–8, *187*
Reed model and 174–9
separating corporate and charitable
activities/letting the charity
board make the decisions
about 161, 173–4
strategic goals of business and
161, 173–4
stakeholders 21, 43, 64, 70–1, 74,
80, 81, 97, 99, 174, 195–6,
198, 201
Standard and Poor's 500 index 91
Stapelstein 105–8, *106*
state support, inequality and
inevitable drop in 56, 57
steward ownership/companies 20,
105, 107, 108, 120, 130, 131,
151, 208, 215. *See also* PhilCo
Stockert, Markus 4, 5–6
Strategic Report 71
Suleyman, Mustafa 46
super-foundation 19

Task Force on Climate-related
Financial Disclosures 70
tax 3, 11, 36, 45, 60, 143, 171, 200,
201, 202, 208, 214
Gift Aid 146, 169, 180, 214
Laffer Curve 55
Tax Reform Act, US (1969) 98
Thatcher, Margaret 43
Toyota 75
Toys 'R' Us 99
trust 81, 106, 112, 141, 189, 196, 213
in business 47, 49
in governments/elected officials 196
trusts, charitable 45, 58, 151, 183, 214
trustees 97–98, 163, 174, 187, 209

choosing 165–68
crossover between directors of the
business and 142
paying 150
Reed Foundation 142, 145
resisting a takeover 102–3

UK Youth 131
Unilever 96
United Nations (UN)
Global Compact 79
Paris Agreement, UN goals to
reach net zero by 2050,
set out in 76
Sustainable Development
Goals 70
Who Cares Wins report (2004) 67

Viability Statement 70
virtual charity 178
Volkswagen 'Clean Diesel'
campaign 81
voting rights 98, 103, 105, 129, 154,
159, 215
vulture capitalism 25, 215

Wang 91
water industry, UK 43
Waterman Jr, Robert H. 91
Wegovy 103, 161
Which? 151
whitewashing 80–1, 215
Whymper, Edward 4–5
Wilsdorf Foundation 123
Wilsdorf, Hans 123
Womankind Worldwide
25, 174–5
worker welfare 41
World Economic Forum (1999) 79
World Fund 121

Zeiss, Carl 151, 153

ABOUT THE AUTHOR

James Reed is a battle-hardened business leader and charity organiser. He became CEO of recruitment company Reed in 1997 and is now one of the UK's longest-serving chief executives. As chairman of trustees at the charity Big Give, James has become the driving force behind Europe's pre-eminent charity fundraising platform.

While James studied at Oxford University and Harvard Business School, he likes to say that he learned more from his father, Sir Alec Reed. Alec founded Reed in 1960 in his hometown of Hounslow with just £75. In the following years, the company has only seen two chairmen – Alec and James. Both men had near-death experiences in their early 50s. Like his father, James Reed combines a can-do approach with a passion for people and new ideas. Karma capitalism is one of these ideas, potentially the best yet.

James has written other books, most notably the best-sellers *Why You: 101 Interview Questions You'll Never Fear Again*, *The 7 Second CV* and *Put Your Mindset to Work*. He also makes regular appearances on television, radio and in the press, as a sought-after commentator on the jobs world and the economy more widely. In 2024, James launched his own podcast series for entrepreneurs, *James Reed: all about business*.

James is married to Nicola and they have six children.

Praise for *Karma Capitalism*

'James Reed is this country's leading voice on effective, strategic philanthropy. His new book is both a persuasive argument for the PhilCo movement and a call to arms for entrepreneurs and executives who want to make the world – and their own companies – a better place. Read it, then go and put his ideas into action.'
– Edwin Smith, editor-in-chief of *Spear's Magazine*

'If you believe, as every successful business leader should, that giving back must be baked into your DNA, then James Reed provides the recipe.'
– Dame Irene Hays, owner and chair of Hays Travel

'Now that I've read this book, I cannot unsee the potential and necessity of Karma Capitalism and the concept of a PhilCo. I will be building these ideas into my business from day one.'
– Sharmadean Reid MBE, founder, creative consultant and advocate for women's empowerment

'Businesses (when they're not cheating you out of your pants) have the power to transform and support our society for the better and James Reed's insightful book tells us exactly how. I know him personally and believe these ideas could lead the way.'
– Ruby Wax, comedian, performer and bestselling author

For more information on Big Give:

For more information on PhilCos: